Order this book online at www.trafford.com/06-0861
or email orders@trafford.com

Most Trafford titles are also available at major online book retailers.

Note for Librarians: A cataloguing record for this book is available from Library and Archives Canada at www.collectionscanada.ca/amicus/index-e.html

ISBN: 978-1-4120-9105-3

www.trafford.com

North America & international
toll-free: 1 888 232 4444 (USA & Canada)
phone: 250 383 6864 ♦ fax: 250 383 6804
email: info@trafford.com

The United Kingdom & Europe
phone: +44 (0)1865 722 113 ♦ local rate: 0845 230 9601
facsimile: +44 (0)1865 722 868 ♦ email: info.uk@trafford.com

10 9 8 7 6 5 4 3

THINK ONLY WHITES ARE RACIST?

THINK AGAIN!

A Black man's Perspective

BY MOHAMMED ALI

For my beloved mother, Salamat, to whom I owe so much.
May God bless her soul.
And
For my beloved father, Suraz, who recently passed away. I miss him.
May God bless his soul.

This is a work of non-fiction. Every episode described in this book is true. The narratives are all real. For incidents occurring in Germany and elsewhere, I changed the names of some of the individuals either for their protection or for legal reasons. Otherwise, all persons mentioned in this book are real.

TABLES

Class of Immigration by Top Ten Source Countries, 2004

PREFACE

Throughout my life, I have experienced racial discrimination almost on a daily basis. I am a Black African Muslim, born in Sokode in the state of Togo, which is located in the region southwest of the Sahara desert. My family moved to Ghana in 1974. Since I left Ghana in 1987, I have lived in Saudi Arabia, Germany and Canada. In every one of these countries I have found that racism isn't perpetuated by whites alone – all races are guilty. I have also found that some global events tend to propel the intensity of, and increase the amount of racism.

The monstrous event of September 11th, 2001 is one of these occurrences that didn't help matters. This, in spite of the fact that every year on March 21, the day earmarked by the United Nations as International Day of the Elimination of Racial Discrimination, I see people of all racial background come together in various cities around the world to demonstrate and to make statements condemning racial discrimination. This global declaration amazes me, not because I hate the noble idea of annihilating racism. Nor am I against people from all walks of life demonstrating their beliefs. It's their actual belief that boggles my mind.

The significant elements of these demonstrations are the participants and their targets. Excluding a few whites motivated by self-criticism or political correctness, the majority of the demonstrators are non-whites who usually direct their anger and venom at what they perceive as white racism. The South East Asians, the Chinese, the Hispanics, and African Americans whom I have met all believe that racism is synonymous with white people who victimize them.

However, in my capacity as a political refugee who has shared rooms and apartments and worked with many racial groups in Africa, Asia, Europe and North America, I see it differently. I don't believe in the baloney that only whites are racist. I hope I am not accused of being a white apologist. Yes, whites may have perpetuated colonialism, segregation and apartheid, and been heavily involved in slavery. And yes white supremacy groups, such as the Ku Klux Klan and other Neo-Nazi groups still exist. But is that all there is about racism?

From my personal experience, it isn't white people who have exhibited the most racism towards me – on the contrary, white people have shown me the least amount of racial discrimination. Unfortunately, the people who top the list of dishing out racism are those who normally complain about being the victims. That is why I believe it is a fallacy to say that racism is a white person's thing, especially when this misperception stems from white people dominating the world's geo-politics.

In contrast, my observation and experience throughout my travels and interactions are that most whites, especially those of West European origin, tend to be sensitive and sophisticated with racism issues. They understand the negative impact and take accusations of racism very seriously.

From my perspective, the vast majority of white people resent being labeled "racist," even if they are practicing it. I have also noted that whites tend to be more considerate in corporate offices, government departments and commercial institutions where they are in charge as opposed to non-whites who rule the roost. This has given me a guiding principle of usually soliciting services in a government office or a store from a white person when both a colored and a white person are serving.

In general, white people show great courtesy to people of color, perhaps because they don't want the race card used against them if non-whites don't receive what they want. On the other hand, non whites don't care whether they are called racist or not. Their logic that racism is a white person's thing is deep rooted; therefore, if you call them racist, they treat it as a joke.

No doubt trying to eliminate racial discrimination is an uphill battle. It just can't be done when some groups believe that racism is only white racism. Racism is racism regardless of its origin and who perpetuates it.

If you have any doubts about the gravity of non-white racism, consider the simple example of relationships and marriages between races. Despite all the myths about black-white frictions, it is an observed fact that black-white unions are some of the most common form of mixed relationships today. For instance, although Germany often gets labeled high as a racist nation, it also has one of the largest black-white relationships per capita in the world.

Unfortunately, mixed-race marriages among some racial groups are non-existent. Some racial groups, particularly those from South and Far East Asia, often consider this type of relationship an abomination or a taboo.

Much has already been written about this vast topic. The difference, though, is these books and articles are generally written by people with little or no direct experience in racial discrimination; their works usually are based on hearsay. However, I have felt and experienced racial discrimination.

Think Only Whites are Racist? Think Again!, is a new kind of book aimed at giving all fronts on the racial spectrum a fair shot, and to make them all accountable for their actions, actions which are often detrimental to others. The book is also designed to change the current landscape of this vast topic and to usher in fresh ideas about fighting racial discrimination.

The bottom line is we need to resolve several issues of racism. People of all race, color, and creed must agree and accept the concept that the color of a person's skin is no more significant than the color of his or her eyes. The philosophy, doctrine, teachings and ideology that rate one race and one skin superior and another inferior, must be realistically fought, discredited and abandoned.

We must genuinely recognize that racism is a menace and fight against it like we fight terrorism. Otherwise, racial discrimination will stick with us forever– despite our demonstrations, flyers and placards.

Mohammed Ali

June 21, 2007

ACKNOWLEDGMENTS

Thanks first and foremost to God Almighty for His many blessings. Thanks to my fiancée Aisha and my entire family. Many thanks to my editor Sharon Crawford for making my words sparkle. Thanks to my publisher Trafford Publishing.

Thanks to the Minister of Citizenship and Immigration Canada and Minister of Public Works and Government Services for permission to reproduce Canada's annual Immigration figures and a quote from Janice Charrete, former deputy Minister of Citizenship and Immigration Canada.

Special thanks to my family physician. Hanna Hinnawi, MD, West Way Medical Centre, Toronto; my surgeons: André Gantous, MD, FRCS, St. Joseph's Health Centre, Toronto, Ralph Gilbert, MD, FRCS, Toronto General Hospital. Thanks to my Oncologist, Brian O'Sullivan, MD, FRCPC, Princess Margaret Hospital, Toronto. Thanks to my Immigration Consultant, Sophie, and my attorney, Joel. Thanks also to Warren Sheffer of Hebb and Sheffer Law Firm, Toronto, for vetting some portions of the book.

Finally, I would like to make a disclaimer that none of the people, institutions, and organizations I have thanked bears any responsibility for what I have written. I am indebted and grateful to all those who have let me into their lives. My thanks and apologies to any person, organization and institution that I have forgotten to mention.

Mohammed Ali

TABLE OF CONTENTS

PART ONE
My Personal Journey

PART TWO

My Personal Thinking (Op Ed)

PART ONE

MY PERSONAL JOURNEY

ONE

Outside Africa - The Maiden Journey

I had to get out of Africa. I was finishing my mandatory post-secondary service with the National Service when politics interfered. The leftist government in Ghana was arbitrarily executing and jailing people on bogus allegations. One of these allegations was against the Ministry of Works and Housing in Accra where I worked as a liaison between the Minister and the Service Personnel. Through the course of my work I had developed a close personal relationship with the Ministry's Secretary. This Secretary was the subject of the investigation. I was also opposed to the regime in my homeland and was involved in attempts to boot out the brutal dictator who had forced my family into exile.

So, on a cool Wednesday evening in late May 1987, I began my maiden voyage outside black Africa. As I boarded the Ethiopian Airlines plane at Accra, Ghana, I had mixed feelings. The only place I wanted to go was Saudi Arabia, because I wanted to perform the Hajj Pilgrimage. If I had the wisdom of hindsight, I should have opted for a western country where I could have sought political asylum. I believe I would have been granted it. The plane's destination, however, was Jeddah, Saudi Arabia.

After two stops in Bangui, Central Africa Republic and

Nairobi, Kenya, we landed in Addis Ababa, the capital of Ethiopia and the airline's home base. To our surprise, an airline official told us to board buses which waited outside at the tarmac. The buses took us to Hotel de Afrique, a luxury hotel several miles from the airport. Once we arrived at the hotel, we hoped the airline official would tell us why we were there; but after several anxious hours, he still didn't give us any answers.

However, a few frequent travelers in our entourage did. They said that we were sent to the hotel because the airline didn't have enough passengers to continue on to Jeddah. So, we had to wait until the airline gathered passengers from its various flights to fill the Jeddah flight. Although initially I felt disappointed at the delay, the experience I had during the almost three days in Addis Ababa kick-started my inspiration to write this book.

At the hotel, we were grouped two people per room. As it was also the Muslim month of Ramadan, the hotel staff secured a list of fasting Muslim guests. Their intent was to adjust the timing of our meals to Islamic tradition of eating before dawn and after sunset. After they compiled the list they gave it to us.

However, in practice, this isn't what happened, perhaps because most of the passengers were illiterates, or elderly, or appeared not to have understood the hotel staff or may have just misled them. Some individuals who gave their names as fasting Muslims for meals only before dawn and after sunset, were later found to be eating three or four times daily. They ate before dawn, the time reserved for fasting Muslims, then joined in for a second breakfast with the non-fasting guests, and again for lunch and later for supper.

I believe this happened because Islam permits its followers to postpone their fast if it will interfere and create unnecessary hardships with their travel. The rule also applies to individuals who are sick. So they could have postponed their fast, but neglected to inform the staff, which understandably infuriated the hotel management and staff. I was genuinely sympathetic to the hotel employees' frustrations because of the financial losses and other inconveniences they suffered. I was equally surprised and impressed that they had the foresight to have these plans in place for Muslims. Ethiopia is not a Muslim country, although a substantial number of Muslims live there.

However, I was outraged over what I perceived as their racist attitude. This might shock some readers, because Ethiopians are Africans, too, and the idea of them practicing racism against fellow Africans might seem strange. Before my stop here, I had also thought that way and had regarded Ethiopia as one of the leading African countries sympathetic to Black African struggles. I had also figured that the headquarters of the now defunct Organization of African Unity situated in their capital, Addis Ababa, sealed this brotherhood.

I wasn't alone in my thinking. Even black people in the Diaspora, especially Rastafarians from Jamaica, have great regard for Ethiopia, and consider it their spiritual holy land. It is also well documented that Ethiopia's former head of state, Emperor Haile Selassie was considered one of the champions of Africa's struggles for independence from colonial rule. And last but not least, Ethiopia received support and solidarity from the international community, especially other Africans, during the brutal famine which nearly wiped it out in the 1980s.

But as I would later find in Saudi Arabia and elsewhere, the majority of people in that region – Sudan, Somalia, Djibouti, Eritrea and, of course, Ethiopia, often collectively called, The Horn of Africa – harbor some kind of belief that because they look different physically (some with fair-coloring), than the black people of the Sub-Saharan Africa, they are superior. The majority of people in this region believe that a person's skin color dictates their status in society.

Unfortunately, this ignorance and prejudice has led to catastrophic consequences for the people here, with Black Africans being the main victims.

Back at the hotel, I was concerned with the appearance of about two-dozen passengers in our entourage. Their dirty clothes were an eyesore. Their once-white robes had taken on the hue of mud brown. Clearly, they hadn't seen water for weeks and neither had the bodies wearing them, if the odors of sweat and urine were any indication. The purveyors of these smells also practiced uncontrolled spitting. By all accounts, it was very disgraceful.

As such, some of these passengers were not fit to travel in an airplane. The authorities from their originating airports could have advised these passengers on the importance of keeping clean and neat while traveling. I don't think they would have made it past any European or North American airports.

I wouldn't call that racial discrimination – it has nothing to do with their robes per se or their traditional customs – but has everything to do with lack of personal hygiene, which could have raised health concerns and provided grounds to keep them off the plane. And I wonder why the authorities of their originating countries let them board the plane. These pilgrims presented the face of their country and that face showed dirt and ignorance. This wasn't the only incident. During the next six years when I lived in the Kingdom (Saudi Arabia), in the cities of Jeddah and Mecca, I often saw people with similar appalling dresses in the Hajj terminal at the Jeddah airport

Then there was the theatrical incident in our hotel room the day we arrived. An old man and his wife took over our hotel room after they returned from the restaurant. They had lost their way and believed our room was theirs. When the hotel staff tried to persuade them to leave, the old couple not only refused to do so, but pushed them away. We were all hampered by not understanding each other's language, so we were already communicating by hands and body language. It took a lot of persuasion from the hotel staff and us, with another push from what I will call "Divine intervention" to get the old couple out of our room.

I was also upset with our Ethiopian hosts' attitude. Despite their knowledge that the passengers were multi-national and came from different countries, they considered us as one. Our hosts tossed out derogatory and condescending remarks. For example, if some of the guests spit, the hosts called us all dirty, smelly, jungle people, and gestured with their hands, suggesting we were stupid.

While I was not personally insulted, I was offended because my fellow countrymen or people from neighboring countries were being insulted in an intolerable manner. Our hosts specifically targeted people from the West Africa Sub region (region southwest of the Sahara Desert and along the Gulf of Guinea, on the Atlantic Ocean). They tried to persuade those of us they considered as enlightened to speak to what they termed as "our people."

It is important to note that none of the passengers in our entourage that I know of, spoke Ethiopian but some of the staff spoke English, so that was our medium of communication. There was also a fellow who wanted to be our tour guide and who spoke perfect English. According to the hotel staff, he had lived in the United States, but was deported because he had no legal documents. They warned us to be wary of this man because they believed he had a criminal history. However, we didn't see that. I think that they feared him perhaps because of his heavy American accent and western lifestyle. Or maybe we were just lucky as this fellow did us no harm.

My anger subsided a little on my last day, which was a Friday. Two other fellows and I decided to attend a Friday prayer. Although the nearest Mosque was a few kilometers away, we walked because we figured we could get in some sightseeing. We definitely saw a lot on our way.

The city core was everything I had seen or heard about capital cities. Filth, slums, panhandlers permeated the streets. Gutters were choked with cabbage; children shifted through the refused dumped everywhere. Despite my sadness staring at yet another ugly face of African cities, I was comforted that, after all, these people using offensive language and believing themselves superior to us, were actually not different from anyone else. However, we managed to pick our way through all the squalor and made it to our destination late Friday morning. But even there, in the Mosque, where everyone is expected to be well-dressed to worship, several hundred people wore dirty clothing and smelled.

That Friday evening, when we finally flew from Addis Ababa and arrived in Jeddah, I took a taxi to the Holy City of Mecca to perform Umra, "the lesser Pilgrimage." (Hajj, the other, occurs three months following the fasting month of Ramadan). After my pilgrimage, I decided to stay in the Holy City – the religious hub for pilgrims – and did so for two more years, mostly undocumented. This was where the real struggle and trouble began. As an undocumented alien, I was forced to do a variety of odd jobs. But an opening came three months after my arrival – although it was a circuitous route to get there.

Hajj Pilgrimage time was nearing. This pilgrimage is an annual duty for able-bodied Muslims all over the world, if they can afford it. With over two million pilgrims making the journey each year, the occasion brings an abundance of activities, especially in the tent city of Mina, a suburb of Mecca. Prior to the Hajj, Mecca bustles with preparations. Saudi nationals and businesses recruit workers to get the city ready for the millions of pilgrims. This prep work includes building tents, setting up makeshift toilets, etc. And that's what I was hired to do. It would also lead to a service job at the Islamic Development Bank, a job with precarious racial confrontations.

One evening as I built some of the pilgrimage tents with my friends in Mina, I heard a horn honk close by. I looked around and saw a sleek black Cadillac parked behind us. The driver hit the horn again, then lowered the car's window and motioned to me to approach. I did and we shook hands. "I'm from the Islamic Development Bank," he said.

He was neither white nor black but fair-colored, and in his late twenties or early thirties.

"I have a job for you," he said.

He wasn't offering me a teller's position, but something a little different from the usual duties of a bank. The Islamic Development Bank, with a membership of more than 44 Islamic countries, had a contract from the Saudi government to oversee the slaughter and distribution of hundreds of thousands of sheep, goats, and cows during the Hajj. It was all part of the Sacrificial Meat Project – a huge undertaking of the Saudi Arabian government.

The meat from this project is kept in huge storage facilities and later distributed to poor communities in various countries around the world. Because this task occurred within a limited time frame, the bank employed thousands of temporary workers, namely, butchers, veterinary officers, doctors and, of course, porters to serve their staff in various forms, such as cleaning the residence, serving food, etc. The project continues to this day, but has increased in size as the Saudi authorities have built more slaughterhouses to cater for the project.

But this wasn't exactly what this driver, a Sudanese national, one of the finest I've ever met, had in mind for me.

"Can you get 10 of your friends to come with you to see my boss? He has a special job for you. I will drive you there."

Without delay, I organized ten of my colleagues and we went with him to see his boss at the office of one of the huge slaughter houses in Mina. Indeed the job was special. As I later discovered, the job was not only an easy one, but there was plenty of food to eat and plenty of money to be made. In fact, the money often made within the three-month period was far more than what I could make elsewhere for the entire year. Many people quit their jobs or took vacation during the Hajj period to work with the bank.

Fortunately for me, I maintained a very special relationship with some of the bosses at the bank for the whole period I was in the Kingdom from 1987 to 1994. So, I had the privilege and opportunity of supplying the bank with workers every year during the Hajj. However, it was not a smooth sail. There were incidents. It was sad; while we worked hard we also did so in fear. As undocumented aliens, we had no guarantees that we would not be fired or get arrested at any time. Some people seemed to take pleasure in giving us a hard time with our work. For about four straight years my friends and I endured confrontations with people from the Horn of Africa.

They were always disrespectful and contempt flowed from them like vomit. Their arrogance was like more bile and they poured it on us by refusing to follow our simple instructions, even when these instructions had filtered down from the bank's hierarchy. They didn't co-operate with the routine protocols of showing their IDs before entering the fenced premises.

One evening the people of the Horn's short-sighted behaviour led to an ugly incident in one of the bank's canteens. My colleagues and I had strict guidelines on the times for the bank staff to have their meals and these were posted in front of every canteen entry. We had clear warnings to forbid anyone entry to the canteens after the stipulated times. My bosses were very blunt – no exceptions, not even a person's position, could bend this rule.

On this fateful day, a group of Sudanese bank staff, who repeatedly violated our instruction, decided to raise the stakes by engaging in a deliberate act of provocation to test our resolve. As usual, their motivation was their twofold disrespect for us – we were both black and undocumented aliens. On previous occasions we had little choice but to let them do what they wanted. But now, we were all unlucky as one of my bosses made a surprise visit late in the night and found these Sudanese guys flagrantly breaking the rules. The boss confronted them.

"Oh, the *Tokoronis* let us in," they said. The boss moved them out, and then approached me as leader of the group.

"No one is allowed in the canteen outside of the stipulated hours." He glared at me. "If you or your colleagues ever let this happen again, you will all be fired immediately."

I tried to explain to him about our situation and why I thought the Sudanese were exploiting it and, of course, their arrogance.

"Don't be afraid," he said. "Use force if necessary to remove anyone violating the instructions."

I was in a Catch-22 situation. I didn't want to lose my job and my privileges, but I also didn't want any form of confrontation with the Sudanese guys because they continually threatened to call the police on us. I hoped that they would be reasonable and desist from further provocations to avoid any ugly incidents. But these guys seemed determined to cause my friends and I problems.

At the core of their behaviour was the fact that they didn't recognize us as equals. Not surprisingly, less than 24 hours after my boss talked to them, a couple of them showed up late in the night. They started banging at the main door.

"Don't let them in, no matter what," I said to my colleagues.

"Keep the doors locked; do not open them under any circumstances or else we will lose our jobs."

When the Sudanese fellows realized we weren't going to let them in, the banging of doors and windows escalated to the point of intolerance. The canteen itself was in an underground location, so I went upstairs and confronted them at the main entrance.

"We don't want to eat," they said. "We're thirsty because of the heat. We need some water to drink."

They had used this pretext previously to get in, but this time, I wasn't giving in. An intense standoff followed. Suddenly it shifted.

"Bro…ther…bro…ther…bro…ther," they chanted.

So now, they decided they needed something from us and as we weren't budging, they would align themselves with us. It worked. We struck a deal, restricting them to water. First, they pretended they only wanted to drink water, but then scattered themselves and began moving towards the storage area for the food, fruits and juice. We jumped in and tried to stop them, but they wouldn't listen to reason. They flipped and the air heated up with racial slurs.

"Jinn (evil people)."

"Sheitan (Satan)."

"Haiwan (animals)."

"Kaleb" (Dogs)."

They slung every insult in the Arabic language at us.

We had no choice but to use every means to get them out. At that point we decided we'd had enough. We would remove them by choice and just be prepared for any repercussions. So, we picked them up, one by one, on our shoulders and flung them outside. Their racial insults increased in vocabulary and noise, but we kept tossing. We did what we needed to do and had no regrets, showed no remorse and shed no tears.

Outside, they looked dejected, embarrassed and disgraced; they left with their tails between their legs. We anticipated that they would call the police, so we stayed alert. To our surprise they didn't, perhaps because it might cost them their own jobs with the bank. There was also no guarantee that if called, the police would take any action against us. The Bosses of the Bank, who were prominent Saudis, could also have protected us from the police. Additionally, it was Hajj time and the authorities knew many illegal immigrants attended the Hajj activities. Except for serious security breaches, the police normally didn't take action against illegal immigrants during the Hajj, particularly at the Holy places.

The following morning, though, the door crashers arrived with one of their own, a man who happened to be senior staff at the bank. As mentioned earlier, they held the mindset of superiority to Black Africans; therefore, they couldn't understand how black guys, particularly those who were undocumented and non-permanent staff of the bank, should have any authority over them.

However, armed with authority from the overall boss who was a real Saudi with massive influence, I approached their boss.

"We did what we were instructed to do," I said. "We did what we needed to do to preserve our integrity and dignity and also to uphold our instructions." I felt empowered. "We have no regrets for what we did and if we have to, we'll do it again."

They all wore a sheepish look on their face. Their boss remained silent. Again they shuffled out in disgrace.

TWO

Mecca - The Wicked and Racist Employer

During my two years in the Holy City, I suffered another incident with vicious racist undertones. I used to sit on specific streets in the city, particularly the *Shara Shetinn* (60th Street) and *Shara Manshoor* (Manshoor Street). These streets were hubs for the city's undocumented people to congregate and solicit work. We'd sit around, talk and wait for Mecca's residents to show up and hire us to do odd jobs – construction, cleaning, wedding preparation. One afternoon as I sat on a bench on Manshoor Street, a Turkish building contractor chose three of us to work on one of the buildings he was constructing.

Because it was during the fasting month of Ramadan, construction work was done mainly at night. I worked for this contractor for almost two weeks but I should have quit on day one. Besides the racist slurs and taunts directed constantly at me, this fellow's other actions should have sent up alarms. He changed workers every day. Unlike most Saudi Arabian businesses, he didn't buy food for his employees. He also didn't drop me home after work, which again most employers did so undocumented workers didn't have to walk home or take public transit and run the risk of being caught by the police.

If I figured all that was bad, I still had the worst to look forward to. About 10 p.m., exactly, on my 14th day, we were manually mixing cement, sand and gravels for the pillars. Unfortunately, I stepped on a four-inch nail, jammed in one of the many pieces of wood we were using for reinforcement and scaffolding. Blood poured from my foot and I was in a lot of pain – physical and mental. The latter was fear about being taken to the hospital where authorities would arrest me and deport me.

I needn't have wasted my time worrying about that. My boss and his colleagues were too busy tossing racial slurs at me. They also cursed me in their Turkish dialect, which I didn't understand. But their body language and the tone of their Arabic diatribe suggested they were saying even worse things and blaming me for what had happened. They were saying in Arabic:

"Tokoroni, Muuk maafi (Black man has no brain)."

"Tokoroni Majunun (Crazy Black man)."

Then they asked me if I was a *Hemare* (donkey).

Ironically, the only rational for their furor was my boss's dread of facing prosecution if my situation worsened so they had to take me to the hospital and the authorities found out they were hiring illegals. I don't know whether they would have taken me to the hospital, but if my situation had worsened, I would have gone myself. And then somebody at the hospital would have alerted the authorities.

There were several instances where African embassies intervened to get Medicare for their countrymen with the guarantee to make them available for deportation when they were cured. Some embassies also took some employers to task, especially employers such as this Turkish man. But Medicare came at a cost. One had to be ready for deportation in case of litigation. I guess I was lucky in that my injury didn't turn worse.

However, the bad didn't stop there. My boss wouldn't pay me for any of the 13 days that I worked for him. So I wasn't surprised to find out that this was his habit. Of course, due to my injury, I was forced to stay home for several days. However, after my recovery, I went to his office on numerous occasions for my money, but every time his administrative assistant told me a different story – he wasn't available, he was in a meeting, etc. – and could I come back later?

Later for me was one morning as I solicited for work on Manshoor Street. My boss stopped by to choose some workers. As was the custom when a vehicle stopped here, a few guys surrounded his car. Initially I thought they were looking for a job, but as I made my way to his van, I heard loud voices and saw fists raised.

"Give me my money. *Yah! Harameen* (a person engaged in prohibited acts)," they chanted almost in unison.

"You hired me last month and you never paid me," another one said.

Then it all clicked in. I put this scenario with the modus operandi of my boss as I had seen him behave previously. Everyday he picked different workers from different locations. He drove slowly beside the sidewalk, stopped, stared at the faces of the people, then moved forward a few meters, again doing the stop and stare routine. He repeated this number five to ten times. Sometimes he just left without picking anyone up.

After today's exhibition, I knew this latter movement meant he had seen people he owed some money. And he didn't always show up himself; often he sent different people driving different cars or sometimes a van.

Because our soliciting spots often stretched over a

kilometer, he varied picking his victims from the beginning, middle or end of the street. He also had the advantage of choosing his victims because we sat soliciting for work in several places in the city. He picked his victims from one street and didn't revisit that street until several weeks or months later. He reasoned that his victims probably wouldn't be around or recognize him by the time he returned. The men who knew him (and his reputation) did not approach him when his car halted. Except today when their need and anger pushed aside any rationalization to stay clear.

So on this particular morning, after an intense standoff, he asked us to get in the van and he would take us to receive our payments. I entered the van along with the other men. But after a few kilometers, we realized he was headed in the direction of a police station. We started screaming and pleading with him to stop and let us out and we would take whatever money he had on him as payment of his debt. He refused. He kept on driving and hurling his trademark cursing and racial slurs at us.

Fortunately, he became stuck at a red traffic light. We mustered our collective energy, pushed the back door open, and stampeded out of the van. We ran helter-skelter, creating a spectacle. In most areas of the Holy City, particularly where heavy concentrations of illegal aliens existed with police and other security agents chasing them, we wouldn't have been an uncommon sight.

Other residents would guide us on the best route to take. But here, in this high-class residential area of rich Saudis, we were a seven-day wonder. The people here had no idea why we were running – they might think we had committed a crime. Also our running track in and out of the cars moving slowly in traffic caused loud and random honking of horns. The drivers were amused and perplexed.

Our goal was to make sure that the police not only didn't see us, but wouldn't find out what was happening. We couldn't risk a police patrol in the area or someone calling the police. But because we numbered 12 and were black in an all Arab area, we stood out.

So, we decided to break into small groups of two or three and take different routes.

Within minutes of our splitting up, a couple of police cars arrived and chased us from street to street and corner to corner. From that moment it was each man for himself. Some of us were unfamiliar with the area and had no idea how to get home. Every time I managed to make it to a distant street and believed I was safe, another police car would surface and head towards me.

As the hide-and-seek with the police continued, I managed to sneak into a house and conceal myself under a staircase, something that was potentially dangerous. On the street I would have been subjected to deportation only because I was undocumented. On the other hand, if discovered here in this house, I would face several other charges.

My worse fear while I was in hiding was to avoid being seen or coming into contact with a female person. No matter what my purpose or intentions were, simply put, I would have been charged with attempted rape, which could result in the death penalty.

While hiding there for almost two hours, my mind dwelt on the universal rules I followed, as did all undocumented aliens. Failure to obey them was at our own peril. For example, it wasn't advisable to take a taxi, public transport run by the Saudi Public Transport Corporation (SAPTCO) or the privately-operated mini buses called "Allagyan."

The reason was simple. Most of the taxis were driven by the secret police, and the possibility loomed of an undocumented person landing at a police station instead of his intended destination. The other two modes of transport were dangerous because the police randomly boarded the buses to check IDs and constantly mounted checkpoints for the same purpose. Our choice of transport, however, was something called Limousine in the Kingdom.

Foreign migrant workers often drove the limousines. Therefore, it was easy to tell the drivers your status and direct them to do your bidding if they saw a checkpoint ahead or to change course if they found a police car close by. They listened if you demanded they drop you off even near a checkpoint. On the other hand, a taxi driver would automatically lock the cars doors and take you to the checkpoint. That was our golden rule and the seasoned undocumented aliens passed it along to the new ones as soon as they arrived. Another rule was to avoid having two or more blacks in a single limousine, because once the police saw two or more black people in a single limousine, they either stopped or chased the vehicle.

We also had another important piece of advise – always try and stay close to the numerous mountains and hills in the Holy City, whether at work or on the street looking for work. Mecca is one of the most mountainous cities in the world, and because being chased by the police was a daily routine once the chase began, all you wanted to do was to try and get to the top of a nearby mountain. Once there, the police never followed, unless of course you were a hardened criminal. Sometimes they lay in wait at the bottom of the mountain for a while.

However, usually, they left after a few minutes. Other aliens told me they didn't pursue us to the mountaintop because they feared rocks would be thrown at them. I understood some of our predecessors used to throw rocks at the police when they chased them to the mountains.

But I crouched under a staircase now and couldn't stay there forever. When I felt it was safe enough to make a move, I crept out of my hiding place and out of the house. As I made my way, I didn't take any chances. I kept vigilant, with my eyes metaphorically set at 360 degrees looking all around me so that I could react in a moment's notice. The fear of deportation when I was unprepared for it gave me many anxious moments.

Luck must have been with me. I tripped through the front door of my residence. I was out of breath but safe for the moment. It was a dire situation; I could well have been deported when I wasn't prepared for it. It definitely would have been catastrophic for me, considering the fact that I had at the time just returned from recuperating from my foot injury.

THREE

Jeddah – Arab Racial Slurs

After this incident, I decided to move from Mecca to Jeddah, Saudi Arabia's biggest city. A few days after my arrival I obtained a job at a scrap metal company. Here, the majority of the workers came from Yemen, Sudan, Somalia, and Egypt. Right away, naming calling became the order of the day. Despite my name being simple and easy to pronounce, these people preferred to call my black friends and I several derogatory names, such as *Tokoroni*, *Aswad*, and *Samara.* Tokoroni is used mainly in the Arab Gulf states, particularly Saudi Arabia, to refer to a black man.

My understanding is that it is not an Arabic word, which explains why it is not used in Egypt, Syria, Jordan, Iraq or Lebanon. Tokoroni is similar to Nigger, as is Samara, which is used mainly in Egypt to refer to a black man. On the other hand, Aswad means "black" in Arabic. However, the manner in which all three are used, especially the laughter that follows, makes them derogatory. And I will certainly take offence if an Englishman who knows my name makes a habit of calling me a black man or Nigger.

The sad side of this entire episode was that although some of these people have light skin and think of themselves as superior to black people, they are universally regarded as blacks. However, their ignorance and prejudice was mind-boggling. Throughout my travels, the Middle East was the only place I found where people have the luxury of calling black people names based on the color of their skin without fearing any consequences.

One guy in particular who insulted me was a walking structure of funny inconsistencies. He had the same name as I, Ali; however, he never called me by name. When he wanted to get my attention, he opened his mouth and screamed at the top of his voice,

"Yah! Tokoroni, taale hina." ("Hey! Black man, Come here.")

Then his peers laughed at me. I scratched my head and pondered the contradictions of his taunts. I'm black, but this guy's skin was much darker than mine.

Perhaps his attitude came from his own inferiority about his citizenship. His colleagues maintained that he was a Kenyan, but he denied that like it was worse than being a criminal. He always claimed Somali citizenry and origin. Why did he think Somalis were better than Kenyans, especially at that time when a vicious civil war was going on in his presumed home country where human suffering of enormous proportion was unfolding?

Somalia has been at war with itself, its neighbours and the international community for well over 30 years. First, it had an uneasy relationship with its main three neighbours; Kenya, Djibouti and Ethiopia. Ethnic Somalis in these three countries desired to be allied with Somalia proper and Somalia claimed territory in those countries – leading to ongoing tension. The situation eventually escalated to a shooting war from 1977-1978 with Ethiopia, in which Somalia suffered humiliating defeat. The hostility, which was known as the Ogaden War, occurred because the ethnic Somalis in the Ogaden region of Ethiopia wanted alliance with Somalia proper to form Greater Somalia.

In January 1991, the then dictator, Siad Barre, who had led them to that war, flew the capital of Mogadishu as rebel forces approached. Hell then broke lose. Ethnic clans began jostling for power. Two war lords, Ali Mahdi and General Farah Adid, emerged as the main antagonists. There was no central government. After months of brutal tit-for-tat attacks, which inflicted heavy civilian casualties on the already impoverished country, the international community intervened by sending peacekeepers. Later, General Adid was seen as the main obstacle to all peace efforts in the country.

For this reason the then Bush (Senior) administration sent in special U.S. troops to capture or kill him. The Americans paid a heavy price for going after one man. As the Americans intensified their search for Adid, so did the intensity of the anti-American, anti-foreign sentiment in the country. Americans were horrified when a Blackhawk helicopter they were using in some of their operations was shot down.

Not only were 18 American Special Forces members killed, their bodies were mutilated and dragged through the streets of Mogadishu. President Clinton, who by then had assumed office, immediately withdrew the American troops. (The incident, by the way, led to the filming of the blockbuster movie *Black Hawk Down*). The U.N, which was also suffering enormous casualties, withdrew. General Adid later died, but was replaced by his son who was in the American military.

Unfortunately, since the overthrow of Siad Barre, Somalia has not had a central government. To make matters worse, a rebel group, which took over the northwestern area of the country, declared it an independent republic of Somaliland.

Since its declaration though, no country has recognized it.

One of my work supervisors, who were himself a Somali, told me Ali didn't want to be linked to Kenya because that country is Black African; therefore, if he came from there, it meant he was Tokoroni, too. This mistaken mentality continues today. I still meet Somalis and people from the Horn of Africa who believe they are superior to the people from the Sub-Saharan Africa. Part of his justification for calling us Tokoroni was based on appearance.

"I and other Somalis have long pointed nose and soft curly hair," he said, while directing a finger to these particular parts of his head. "This isn't the case with black people." It became his trademark every time we met.

Funnier than his trademark was the rest of his appearance. He could give Michael Jordan competition in height but the rest of his torso was like a second-rate skeleton. His face was not something you would want to see in a mirror – protruding teeth and a huge forehead. Up close he looked like a poster boy for an incurable disease. My colleagues used to counter his racist taunts by calling him an AIDS patient. But the guy was so obsessed with his prejudiced beliefs; he didn't care what we said about him. Seriously though, the fellow was a sick human being, in mind and body. I often wished he would concentrate on seeking medical help instead of this preoccupation with racist taunts and slurs.

He wasn't the only person at the scrap metal company who harboured these off-kilter beliefs. All the fellows from Yemen, Sudan, Somalia and Egypt thought the same way. The only difference was, the lanky guy with the protruding teeth broadcasted his feelings loud and clear about us. They say, empty barrels make the most noise, and obviously this guy was one.

From the scrap heap I soon moved up to drugs – the

legitimate kind obtained by semi-legitimate means, i.e., Jeddah's version of sidewalk job soliciting. One morning as I sat there, a friend from the Jos state of Nigeria walked over to me and informed me that a car containing two Southern Nigerians was parked in the distance. It appeared that these two men from a pharmaceutical company were looking for fellow southerners who had a residence permit.

"Permit" here means fake because none of us hanging around here soliciting for work had the original documents. Generally, it was difficult to secure a Saudi Arabian residence permit, so we knew that the van guys were not looking for people with genuine Saudi documents. Obviously, anyone with proper documents would not sit by the roadside and solicit for work. Fake documents were expensive to obtain, so only a few people spent their precious money to secure them. The reason the van guys asked for people with documents is because, of course, they couldn't ask for people without papers.

The idea was that potential employees didn't tell prospective employers they carried fake documents. Once they were hired, if the authorities caught them working without proper documentation, their employers could defend themselves by claiming they had no knowledge of any fake documents.

However, on this day, I decided to act on my friend's tip and forced myself inside the van. As I sat down, the dozen or so guys inside gave me a dirty look, directed particularly at the three tiny tribal marks on my cheeks. They are the way African tribes, mostly in West Africa, identify their ethnic backgrounds and are our version of a birth certificate. As most northern Nigerians have these marks, the fellows in the van jumped to the wrong conclusions. I could feel the animosity before they spoke.

"You son of a bitch? Why did you bring us a Hausa man, a

Northerner? People who can't even speak English." They spoke over my head to my Nigerian colleague. They shook their fists at him and one grabbed his collar.

"Tell me, you dunderhead," one of them asked. "Why bring to us a Hausa *mummu?*"(Southern Nigerian slur for uncivilized or illiterate person).

And on and on it went, with me sitting like the invisible man in the backseat of the van. I knew that their outrage stemmed from the centuries of bitter rivalry between their two ethnic groups.

Nigeria has three dominant tribes out of the more than one hundred. The Hausas, who are mainly Muslim, are in the north; the Ibos, who are predominantly Christian, are mostly in the southeast; the third group, the Yurobas, who dwell in the southwest, are 50-50 Muslim and Christian. The Ibos and the Hausas were involved in a brutal war, the Biafran War, in the 1970s, a war in which the Ibos wanted to break away from the Federation.

While a few Ibos still pursue independence, religious dissension has taken over the politics of the Hausas and Ibos. In the past couple of years, tit-for-tat attacks between the two groups occurred because of religion, killing several thousand people on both sides. On the other hand, the Yurobas remained in the middle. However, no love is lost between the Yurobas and the other two groups.

While being called a northerner in other parts of the world is no problem, it is a big deal in Ghana, Togo, Benin, Ivory Coast and Nigeria. People from the north of these countries are largely Muslim, poor, and uneducated. So the word "northerner" is often used to insult people from the northern part of these countries.

Despite this background of dissent in the van that day, I managed to keep my cool and never uttered a word. I also avoided speaking English, perhaps partly from a perverse wish to go along with their mistaken assumption about me, but more for what I could only call a personal victory. If I had done something stupid, with the possibility of severe implications for them, I'm not sure how I could have kept my sense of integrity.

As the only Muslim in the group, and knowing that they had all changed their given names to Muslim names to let them work in the Kingdom, I could have simply reported them to the Mutawahs (the Kingdom's morals police). This would lead to their detention and deportation. But thank God, I didn't do it.

Meanwhile, the two Nigerians already working for the company wanted to get rid of me, so they had the driver take them to their residence where they picked up three of their colleagues who wanted work.

From the talk in the van, the company needed 10 workers, but there were now 15 of us already in the van, excluding the two Nigerians and the driver, a company representative. If more men than the number required by the company showed up, the company dropped some of them. The two Nigerians urged their colleagues to be smart and fast, and to stay in front of me if we queued to enter the company. Then, if the employers decide they needed only 10 people, I would not be able to enter.

After about 30 minutes, we arrived at the company's main gate. The hustling and jostling for the positions began. Again I kept my composure and decided to stay at the tail of the queue. As we entered, the gate guards issued cards to each of us, no questions asked. We entered the building without delay and were given our various assignments.

As casual labourers, we were usually paid after the day's work and told not to come back if our services were no longer needed. But to our surprise, we were not paid at the end of the day, but instead were told to return the following day. This continued for a week.

Unfortunately for me, I got sick on my fifth day and couldn't work. Incidentally, this was the day the company had decided to lay off all but four of our contingent. Although I did not work that day, my employers decided to keep me. Within a couple of weeks I became the management's "favourite son," and sooner than expected, they elevated me to group leader. This group included the guys who thought I was illiterate and didn't want me to be employed in the first place. And for all this I did receive pay.

From the day of my elevated position, our roles were reversed – I became their boogieman. And more surprises came along for them. First, our chief engineer called me aside and secretly asked me to get ten of my hard-working friends and bring them to work. I said nothing to my Southern Nigerian friends.

After two days of intense search, I managed to gather my favourite friends and brought them in. My Nigerian friends hit a ten on the anger scale. The next morning they marched with their friends to the company's gate. They demanded that their friends be hired. However, the Personnel Manager had other ideas – he warned them to leave the company premises or he would call the police.

Meanwhile, as time passed, my Nigerian friends and I agreed on a truce. We found it was necessary because we needed each other to fight the real problem – the huge number of Filipinos, Pakistanis, East Indians, and Egyptians in the company who constantly aimed racial slurs, insults and curses at us. There were about hundred Filipinos, while the Pakistanis and East Indians had hundred employees between them, about fifty Egyptians, not to mention the Bangladeshi's, the Sudanese, etc. It was an uphill task working in this environment.

As I mentioned in the introduction, these people are the ones who play both sides of the racism fence. When the racial slurs hit them, they claimed they were victims, but when it was convenient for them, they perpetuated racism on their own. This is where I see the hypocrisy, which makes me question who are the racists and who are the real victims? I wish I could remember all the racial slurs the different racial groups have used against me so I could write them in this book. Then you would have a better idea of what I am up against.

The sad part of the whole situation is that some of the people whom I considered good friends often exploited my innocence and used a racist slur, but they told me it meant a greeting or a good word in their dialect. Later I found out differently. A young Filipino, Mario, taught me the Philippines Tagalong dialect. At one point it seemed as if I were more fluent in Tagalong than Arabic.

Because of Mario's closeness to me and my black colleagues, his countrymen disliked him and called him a homosexual, a huge insult in the mainly Roman Catholic Philippines, and in Saudi Arabia, where homosexuality can lead to the death penalty. Some times my Nigerian friends and I learned the words were bad when, thinking they were good, we called them back. On one occasion, a Filipino friend told me I was *Butagenamo.* He told me it meant "a nice guy." However, when I checked with Mario, he told me it was a bad word meaning "son of a bitch."

The East Indians were also calling my all-black group of workers, *Gondo Group.* At first we were told it meant "a good group." But we later learned it meant "fucking group." Every Indian I subsequently asked confirmed it indeed meant "fucking group."

However, fortunately my Nigerian friends and I managed to find what I call "unlikely allies," to the surprise of our East Indian, Pakistani, Filipino and other colleagues, who considered themselves superior to black people. Our high profile company had connections with businesses in Germany and Italy and imported most of their machines from them. These European firms usually sent their own engineers and technicians to install or repair our machines. Every time they came, my black brothers and I had good rapport with them. We could connect through conversations about Africa, soccer, and other issues amid jokes, laughs and hugs. And our prejudiced friends noticed.

After all was said and done, our supposedly "superior" friends came to us, wanting to know what we were talking about and expressing surprise that we could manage a friendly, racist-free relationship with the Europeans.

Generally, over the years, I observed that these people who hurled racial slurs at us were actually timid and had an inferiority complex in the vicinity of white people. I believe this explains their cynicism about white people and their allegations of suffering discrimination. At the same time, I can see how they would turn around and act racist towards any group they considered inferior to them. If there is a pecking order in racism, this is a good example of it.

By the way, the racism wasn't just against my African brothers and me. As a matter of observed fact, there were constant racial tensions among these other groups, too. The East Indians and the Pakistanis felt they were superior to the Filipinos and vice versa. The Egyptians, the Lebanese and other Arabs felt they were superior to all the rest and vice versa. And they all engaged in mutual name calling. When I was with a Filipino, he told me what was wrong with an Indian or Chinese or Arab. When I was with an Arab, he told me the same thing about the Filipino and others, and so on. However, no matter what their differences, they all believed in one common philosophy – superiority over black people.

In the meantime, my struggle with racism was not limited to my place of work. Back home in my block lived a wicked black-hater named Ibrahim. This fellow, a Saudi of Yemeni extraction, had a flat in a one-storey building opposite my residence.

He was so isolated that for the two years I lived in the neighbourhood, I never saw anyone else living with him – no children, no women, not a single family member. He was always alone. And he never seemed to work. He spent his time spying on my colleagues and me. The house where I lived had an open compound so he had no trouble seeing most of the activity down below.

On several occasions I could see him standing on the flat concrete roof, leaning over the three-to-four-foot fence surrounding it, and staring down at my place. Other times, he sat in front of the entrance to his building, which was also directly opposite my own entrance, and watched whatever moved in and out. For years, I was suspicious of his motives and intentions. However, I felt the only reason he hadn't acted against me was because he thought I was a legal resident. Or may be it was just luck.

However, he had vicious plans and he unleashed them sooner than I thought he would.

On a clear sunny Friday in 1993, Ibrahim shocked the entire neighbourhood when he caused the arrest and deportation of forty of our boys. We had all returned to Jeddah after soothing our souls and lining our pockets from the Hajj Pilgrimage in Mecca. Usually, we spent the next few days resting before returning to our routine jobs. This time, however, some of my friends had bought stereo equipment.

So, Friday, following the afternoon prayer saw us relaxing, listening to music and watching videos, played low, because in Saudi Arabia, no one could turn the stereo or TV up high without getting charged with a noise violation. Unfortunately for these guys, the nature of their residency and their mode of living made it easier for mass arrest. We shared the same landlord and only a corridor separated us.

But there the similarity ended. My residence contained two normal bedrooms. One bedroom was mine and my two roommates shared the other one. However, the other forty guys had six bedrooms, formerly classrooms in a school converted to a residence. They had no beds and slept on mattresses because that made space to crowd more people into the rooms. These guys had arrived in Jeddah within the last two months to a year. I had started my humble residency the same way, but as I became more established with work, the number of roommates I had to live with dwindled. This was the norm.

So on this day, a young lady whose brother was our "illegal alien" photographer came with this brother to visit the forty guys – purpose: to take photographs; insinuation from Ibrahim: prostitution.

Ibrahim was doing the male version of the woman scorned – previously he'd tried to seduce the young lady but she'd pushed him away. Now Ibrahim complained to the morals police that a young lady was having sex with forty guys in a male residence. Within minutes, an old model GMC SUV drove up and parked in front of the main entrance, blocking the only escape. The police poured out of the vehicle, entered the residence and picked up the guys, one by one, for deportation.

The entire episode sent shockwaves throughout the neighbourhood. The solidarity among Saudis, Africans,

Egyptians, etc. to this unprecedented arrest was overwhelming. Usually the police apprehended one to three people at a time, and on the streets, not in the residence.

The overall atmosphere was sombre. Some Saudis wept, because most of these guys washed their cars, and they knew them well. They knew the guys were not criminals. They were mere car washers. The Saudis figured the fellows were people they called *Miskin*, ("poor people") who earned their daily bread by washing cars only to help themselves and their poor families back home.

Ibrahim continued his random rampage of getting our boys arrested. He falsely accused my former roommate of stealing his air conditioner. When Ibrahim found the accusation false, he was instrumental in getting this man deported. So, it was no surprise to me that I was his next target a few months after the deportation of the forty.

At that time, I had a girlfriend, a Nigerian beauty queen named Jenny, who was Ibo. She lived in a different area of the city and visited me on weekends, which are Thursdays and Fridays in the Kingdom. Although we tried to keep ourselves scarce from Ibrahim, there was no doubt that he knew Jenny visited me. However, he couldn't have known her race. Jenny had fair skin and she always wore *Abaaya*, the black dress worn by Saudi women which shows only their hands and face. Ibrahim probably figured that she was an Arab girl.

One Friday morning, as I had my breakfast with Jenny and her cousin, Adana, who had arrived a day earlier from Nigeria, I heard a noise coming from my roommates. It sounded as if someone was headed to my room. I heard my friends say *"Maafi, Maafi,*" in Arabic, ("No one is there, no one is there.") Before I could act, I saw my door slowly open to reveal a uniformed man. Jenny became hysterical, murmuring, cursing and talking erratically, while I tried to convince her not to give the officer reasons to be more belligerent.

She had warned me to move to her place after the mass deportation of our colleagues, and had threatened not to visit me again if I failed to move. But this was not the time for talk. It appeared that the die was cast and there was no way we could escape. After all the near misses, I knew my days in the Kingdom were over.

The police officer looked around quickly. I thought he was going to draw his gun, but instead he started dancing to the music from the video. He picked up a glass on top of the centre table and swallowed most of it, then made a face.

"Aargh. Water," he scowled at me. "Give me some whisky."

"Sorry," I said. "No booze here. I don't drink." I lowered the volume.

"Pump it up. Pump it up. I want to dance with her." He pointed to Jenny.

At this point, I realized his intentions. I turned to Jenny, sitting beside me on my bed. She leaned towards me. Her cousin over on the sofa across the room, sat like she was fast frozen. Her mouth stood open and her fingers clutched the arm of the sofa.

"I want to dance with her," the policeman repeated. "She's nice, just my color."

"No," said Jenny. Her voice shook.

The officer turned to me. "I want to have sex with her. I'll give her fifty Saudi riyals afterwards."

"Sorry, but the ladies are both married," I said. "They've only come for a short visit on their way to a cousin's."

"Uh, uh, I know those two are prostitutes." He handed me a set of keys. "They belong to your neighbour who said we can use his place. Take her..." He pointed to Jenny. "...and open the door to let me in. I'll follow and we can have sex."

"No," these ladies are married," I said.

"Don't get smart with me. I know all about you. Ibrahim has told me everything. He said you are with an Arab prostitute."

From the look he gave Jenny and then her cousin, I gather he had figured out she wasn't a prostitute and was having doubts about her cousin, too.

This called for a quick plan on my part.

"Very well," I said. I stood up and looked at Jenny. "But it will have to be here. Jenny, I will have to go." I nodded at her and hoped she would get my drift. If I stayed, he could call the morals police and that could have serious repercussions. In the Kingdom, it was forbidden for unmarried adults of the opposite sex to be in the same room at the same time. However, the police officer could also find himself in even more serious trouble, if he refused to leave after I did, because Jenny and her cousin could raise the alarm that he was there to rape them.

As I left, I muttered to Jenny and her cousin to persuade the officer to leave. All I wanted was to get the hell out of the vicinity. When I bolted outside, I saw Ibrahim and another police officer sitting in a police car. Their heads were turned towards me and they were laughing. I swung round and behind me was the other police officer from my room. I knew my plan had worked. Finally Jenny stormed out with her cousin.

"You idiot. You should have moved to my place after those forty guys were arrested." She placed her hands on her hips. "Now look what's happened. You're moving to my place, today. No arguments."

A few days later I was out of my place and into hers. Months later, I learned Ibrahim had been arrested and jailed on drug charges. No wonder he lived alone and was so paranoid. He was the criminal afraid of going to prison.

My relationship with Jenny, though, was short-lived. Shortly after I moved to her place, she found me a new apartment about six blocks from hers. Because we weren't married, I couldn't stay with her; the landlord wouldn't allow it because it was illegal for unmarried couples to live together in the same apartment. But Jenny visited me and stayed over many more times than I did at her place. One night, however, a small dispute erupted between me and Jenny after she came to my apartment at 10 p.m.

Normally, when she arrived at that time, it meant she would stay the night and maybe a couple more days afterwards. But this time her body language was different because as I began to make romantic moves on her, she protested.

"If I sleep with you I don't want sex. I'm not ready for it," she said. "I'll only stay here if we sleep only. If you want sex, then you have to come with me to my apartment."

I started to protest, but she interrupted.

"No, Ali, I mean it. You are showing me disrespect by not visiting my place as often as I come over here."

She'd pulled this Jenny trick before, but she'd usually give in to me. I would be lying in bed, thinking she'd left, only to see her return to my room, fresh from taking a shower, and then climb into bed beside me. So, I figured she was pulling the same old stunt.

So I continued to try making love moves, but she stood up, walked over to the door.

"Ali, get up and come over to my place."

I thought she was joking, so I buried my head in my pillow and waited for her to take her shower as usual, then come and lie with me. I heard her stamp her foot and looked up to see her scowling at me.

"Ali, if you don't come with me now, I'm leaving and

you're never going to see me again."

Then she left. True to her words, I never saw her again, although I don't think it was her heart's wish that it would go this way.

Meanwhile, we played the wait-and-see-who-would-break-first game. Neither of us contacted the other. Two days later as I rode my bike home from work, a friend of mine who lived at my old place stopped me.

"Ali, do you know that Jenny has been arrested by the police and been taken to the deportation centre?"

"No," I said. "I don't believe it."

"It's true. It's true."

"When was she arrested? For what?"

"I don't know."

"But it can't be," I said. "I saw her only 48 hours ago. How could she have been arrested and her deportation processed so quickly?"

"Ali, it's true." He then directed me to his information source.

Without hesitating, I went to the source and received confirmation of what I had heard earlier. She was arrested while riding in a taxi at one of the city's numerous checkpoints as she returned from shopping in downtown Jeddah. From the source, I went straight to her home. On her door I saw half a dozen notes posted by her girlfriends who had come to visit her. At that moment I knew it was true. All I wanted to do was secure her precious belongings, help get some of them to her so she could take them as her accompanying cargo before her deportation. Thankfully, I managed to get most of her stuff. But her unintentional prophecy that I wouldn't see her again became a reality – I have not seen her since she last left my apartment.

In the meantime, at my work place, the racial tension

between my Nigerian friends and me on one side, and the East Indians and Filipinos, etc. on the other, escalated. Unfortunately, my Nigerian friends were not helping matters. One guy in particular was so arrogant; he refused my advice and over-indulged himself in keeping company with some Arab youths. He was always going out with them, which was dangerous, especially for a black man with fake identity papers.

They say "don't throw stones if you live in a glass house," but that was exactly what he was doing. He was living dangerously because the authorities were always suspicious if they saw a black person with Arab young men. That usually meant they were dealing in or doing drugs. I also feared for my Nigerian friends because they were not Muslims and had only adopted Muslim names so they could secure fake documents and employment. They didn't necessarily have to be Muslims to secure work in the Kingdom, but because they were illegal, it was risky for them to use their non-Muslim names because it might expose them to further suspicions, arrest and deportation.

Another point is, because my Nigerian friends were unfamiliar with many Islamic rituals, such as the five compulsory daily prayers and ablution – the washing of face and hands before prayer, they opened themselves to self-destruction if they hung out with the Arab youths during the fasting month of Ramadan, and thc Arab youths founds the Nigerians eating or not performing the five daily prayers. The Arabs could report them to the morals police; their documents could then be checked; they would not only be jailed for at least nine months, they might also be lashed and get deported after they had served their sentences. So, I believe indulging in friendships that could hurt their interest was unwise.

But somewhere along the line, my suspicions began to show in a wider direction. Not only did these Arab youths begin suspecting that some of us were actually not Muslims, so did the East Indians and the Pakistanis. They had seen my Nigerian friends struggle to perform simple Muslim rituals and talked trash about them during break on the rooftop – the only place without surveillance cameras and where we could take a nap during break. I just tolerated them, because I knew we were all hustlers and I didn't want to do anything to hurt them. However, at some point I became very concerned and kept on the alert for all possible eventualities.

To add to the racial tensions between my Nigerian friends and I, and the East Indians and Pakistanis, the latter two continued to ask me whether my friends were true Muslims. The logic was that if they weren't, their papers were fake. There was no question about my Islamic faith because not only could I perform the Islamic rituals with ease, on a number of occasions I was asked to lead prayers, which I do very well. And my numerous pilgrimages to Mecca left no doubt about me.

Gossip about our documents soon became the order of the day at work. Thanks to all the racial tensions between the South Asians and us, I always feared someone might do something stupid by alerting the authorities. My Nigerian friends were also doing something else disturbing which I advised them was dangerous and could be problematic. But as always, they never took me seriously. My advice here concerned the way we traveled in and out of the company.

Because it wasn't safe for us to use public transport, we decided to bicycle to and from work. I told my friends that we shouldn't travel in formation to work or home because it make it easier for the police on patrol to do on-the-spot ID checks, especially when it involved more than half a dozen black men. But because my friends were once stopped and managed to escape the police detecting their IDs, they thought they were invincible here. They saw no reason to stop riding as a group. For several months they continued to ride together to and from work, while I decided go solo using safe routes. My action drew criticism from them and they labeled me an isolationist.

One afternoon, everything I feared came true. We had finished work and as usual, they traveled in formation on the main road where our South Asian friends also traveled on the bus. As my friends rode along, they saw five police jeeps on the road. Sensing the danger, they ditched their bicycles and began to run. That was their best strategy because they could move into narrow areas where the police could not go with their vehicles. Fortunately, they all managed to escape the police, but not the eyes and attention of our South Asian colleagues watching the scenario from the buses.

When I arrived at work the next morning, I didn't know what had occurred, but I gathered that something was wrong. Murmurs were everywhere, and after our first break a couple of the East Indian fellows approached me and told me what they had seen. Although they concluded that these guys didn't have genuine papers, they kept asking me why they avoided the police. By midday, the incident had spread to all departments, including the personnel department.

From that day on we became the subject of suspicion. Eyes followed us everywhere and mouths gossiped. I felt embarrassed and uncomfortable. Sadly, my Nigerian friends appeared indifferent and did not get the message. They didn't seem to care. The company authorities, too, did not take any action, at least for the next four to five days, which might have explained my friends' confident mood and *laissez-faire* attitude.

About eleven to twelve days after the above-mentioned incident, our troubles increased. On the Monday, as usual we went to the company canteen for lunch. The canteen, which was in a building about two kilometers from the main one, contained the residences for the company's contract workers. Apart from a few workers who traveled in their own cars to the canteen, the rest of us took the company bus.

However, one of the Nigerians, as usual, traveled with the Arabs in their car. As we sat eating in the canteen, we reckoned there was some dispute between this fellow and one of the Arab guys. After lunch, we boarded our buses and headed back to the company. When we arrived at the gates, security stopped us and told us that anyone who was not on contract with the company would not be allowed in.

Security then gave us this advisory from the personnel department: Saudi immigration officials were coming to check identity papers. Because we were non-contract workers and because the company wasn't sure about our documents' authenticity, they had to remove our time cards. Security had orders to prevent us from entering the company's premises.

"Leave now. You can return when everything is settled," one of the security guards said.

But it never happened. Human Resources didn't call us back. Our flirt with the company had ended. For me, personally, it was a big loss because it was the finest company I had ever worked for in my entire life. At one stage, it appeared as if the company would let me stay on, so they delayed paying me my monthly income for over two weeks. The company, however, paid all my friends within two days of the incident because they had decided they wouldn't rehire them.

Meantime, I constantly checked with my company contacts, particularly the maintenance department head and his subordinates. The problem, though, was with the personal department, which had some anxiety about taking me back – they feared it was too risky for the company.

I was devastated. At the time of the incident I had just

begun to have a foothold in the company. I had also just mourned the death of my beloved mother who had passed away less than a month earlier. Because I received news of her death after my family had performed the funeral in accordance with Islamic tradition, which requires early burial, I decided to arrange a memorial service for her here. It was well attended. Before the bicycle incident, my aim had been to continue working for a couple of months and then if the company still needed my services, I would return home and secure proper documents. This way I could enter into contract negotiations with them.

Unfortunately, due to the carelessness and stubbornness of my Nigerian friends, my dream was shattered. On the other hand, our South Asian and Filipino colleagues had a field day as our pain and downfall became their celebration. Racism indeed knows no sympathy.

FOUR

Germany: - Seeking Political Asylum

I landed in Germany December 15, 1995 and received a pleasant shock. The friends meeting me on my arrival advised me to seek political asylum. Mentally I scratched my head. I thought political asylum was reserved for high profile politicians, such as heads of state and cabinet ministers who suffered a military coup. I had no idea that the ordinary person or a low profile political activist who feared persecution in the home country could apply for political asylum and seek protection in safe third countries.

After a brief consultation with a lawyer, I registered the same day as a refugee claimant with the German authorities at a refugee reception centre in Neu Ulm, Bavaria. The centre was a former military camp previously used by the American Military. But German authorities had converted it into a transit centre for screening refugees and conducting interviews and hearing. From there, authorities transferred refugees to various cities, towns and regions across the country.

To my surprise, as well as most of the day's other claimants, the authorities scheduled my hearing for Monday,

December 18, three days after my arrival. As with many refugees, I had turned up in the country with another person's documents. This is perfectly legal under international law. A person escaping persecution or in fear of his or her life can use whatever means necessary to reach a safe destination, provided the action doesn't harm others or the use of the documents aren't for criminal or other nefarious activities. So, I didn't have a single identity paper of my own with me.

Because I was doing the escape shuffle, carrying double ID would have been a bad move that could have landed me flat on the floor. It's something you just don't do and is a golden role for all refugees and asylum seekers. With the authorities giving me two non-business days to scare up my personal documents from Africa, I knew a fair hearing wasn't going to happen. The prospects for the rejection of my claim and immediate deportation seemed inevitable. However, nothing could change the minds of the authorities.

Back at the refugee home, which was located in the same compound as the federal offices, my colleagues were perplexed. They thought I was getting a rough ride, because some of them had been there for months and the authorities still hadn't called them for their hearings. This wait enabled them to secure their personal documents from their home countries and to prepare for their hearings.

So, On December 18, I woke up empty-handed in personal documents but heavy-hearted in anticipation of my hearing. I walked slowly to the *Bundesamt* (Federal Office) where my hearing was scheduled. The clerk there directed me to a waiting room. As I sat twiddling my thumbs and trying to calm my mind, an officer came in with more questionnaires for me to fill out. One question asked what language I would like used in my hearing. During my registration, I had told the authorities that although I was a Togolese National and

French is the official language, I do not speak French. I also told them why. My family was forced to flee to neighbouring Ghana when I was very young, so, I also had almost all my education in that English-speaking country.

Personally, I didn't want to learn the French language because I resented the French authorities. I hated their strangled hold on my homeland and their unwarranted interference, which had allowed one of history's most ruthless and brutal rulers to stay in power for a long time, all at the Togolese people's expense. I also resented that French leaders always tried to impose the French language on others.

I also opposed my country's membership in the La Francophonie because I saw it as a symbol of colonialism and imperialism. French leaders have always tried to convince their so-called former colonies to avoid giving in to English language dominance and culture because they see them as a threat to the French language. However, as we Africans have our own languages and culture, I think the French would be better off encouraging us to save our own languages and cultures instead of telling us to save theirs and imposing their cultural values, language and hegemony on us.

So, I told the German authorities I was fluent in my native language of Kotokoli which is spoken only in central Togo, mainly around my hometown of Sokode. First they thought I was fluent in English but couldn't speak Kotokoli, so they brought in a Kotokoli interpreter. During the exchanges they found out I spoke fluent Kotokoli; the interpreter also was surprised and acknowledged that I spoke the language perfectly. Just before the hearing began, they opted to conduct the hearing in English. I believe they chose English for their own convenience. During the hearing, the Federal Officer bombarded me with questions.

"Are you a terrorist?"

"No," Sir. I answered.

As this line of inquiry continued on and on, it gave me ample opportunity to mull over why this was going on. Of course, it only occurred because I am Muslim.

If I had a Christian name, it wouldn't matter if I were black; the operative word was the religious one and its connotations.

"Christian" meant "good" in his books and "Muslim" meant "bad"

Then the questions about my nationality became a thorny issue.

"Are you a Togolese National?"

"Yes," Sir. I answered.

"Are you sure?" He asked.

"Yes, I' m sure."

I got the picture. Because I didn't speak French, the Officer didn't believe that I was a Togolese National. To make matters worse, the Sierra Leonean interpreter stood up in front of the officer and looked me in the face.

"I've never seen a Togolese national and refugee speak his kind of English." He pointed to me, then turned to the Federal Officer. The Officer frowned and I knew his suspicions of me had just risen a few notches.

So the hearing switched from my fear of persecution to trying to establish my identity. But without sufficient time to get my documents from home, there really wasn't anything else I could do except to hope for a miracle.

I wasn't surprised a few weeks later when my claim was turned down. According to German asylum laws, it was the worse form of rejection. Generally the authorities have two forms of rejection, *offensichlich unbegrunted* (manifestly unfounded), which is the worse kind; the other rejection is *unbegrunted* (unfounded). With the later rejection, your nationality and identity had been determined and even though your claim may be rejected, there is acknowledgment that problems do exist in your homeland and your appeal has a chance of success. In this decision, the appeal deadline is normally two weeks.

However, with the former type of rejection, your identity has not been established; in other words, you are an economic refugee.

Here, you have only one week to appeal. This is difficult because there is always the possibility that your lawyer might not get the paperwork finished before the deadline in most cases, resulting in immediate arrest and deportation. Even if the lawyer meets the deadline, the appeal timeline is no more than three months. The courts have always sided with the Federal Officers' rulings; with *offensichlich unbegrunted* decisions, the courts' verdicts are often swift.

Fortunately for me, the lawyer I found prepared my appeal on time and entered it in the Administrative Court of the city of Augsburg. By federal law, I had the right to ask for a second political asylum while my appeal was pending Through the Bundesamt, I made a new claim from scratch, in writing instead of a face-to-face hearing. This time I was ready because I had most of my IDs mailed to me and I also had the opportunity to give detailed information about my claim. I knew that the first claim was the one that mattered. However, I felt I had been treated unfairly and hoped that cool heads would prevail to understand my situation.

As I sat in the Bundesamt writing my statements, the officer who conducted my first hearing came into the room. His face dropped as if he were ashamed. Every time I looked up from my writing, he turned his head away as if I were damning him. Then he swung around and hurried out the door. Other factors, such as my tribal marks, my assistance to the *Diakonie* as an interpreter and, of course, the documents I submitted later gave the Federal office second thoughts about my nationality, and showed good reason for this officer's conduct – he had made a terrible mistake by rejecting my claim.

Most of the refugee reception centers had social workers' groups who worked independently from the federal officers to assist refugees in various ways. One of these was the *Evangelical Diakonie Werk,* a humanitarian group who assisted refugees in various forms, namely counseling. They also organized small classrooms for beginners in German, and did other social assistance. They acted like a liaison between the Bundesamt and the refugees. Also at the centre was a young pregnant Togolese woman who came from my home region. According to her, she was raped by the Togolese security forces during election-related violence and was forced to flee the country for her life.

Now the significant thing about her was that despite living all her life in Togo, she spoke not a word of French. The only language she knew and spoke was my native Kotokoli. Because of her precarious situation she needed constant help from the Diakonie Werk, but there was no one to assist her in translating her problems to the social workers.

Humanitarian groups, such as the Diakonie Werk and Caritas (a Catholic relief group), unlike the Bundesamt, have limited resources and are unable to recruit interpreters. These groups have to rely on the refugees, expecting them to be fluent in German, English or French. In situations where the refugee cannot speak any of these languages, then attempts are made to get fellow refugees to help in the interpretation business. And there lay the irony. Although over fifty Togolese acknowledged as such by the authorities lived at the centre, most of these Togolese were southerners and couldn't speak Kotokoli.

As this pregnant refugee and the Diakonie Werk staff were struggling to find a translator, they heard about me and the group led by one Frau Mayer approached me for assistance. Without hesitation I offered to help. For the next three months I was always with this beautiful hardworking German blonde, going from hospital to various offices, as we tried to help this poor young lady. At one point, I became both her translator and counselor as she struggled over what to do about her condition – stay pregnant and give up the child for adoption after birth; keep the baby herself, or take the extraordinary measure of abortion.

What a paradox. Here I was the guy who had his claim for asylum turned down solely because he didn't speak his country's official language, now I was the only person in the camp who understood this lady. Word soon traveled to the federal officials about what was happening. Frau Mayer had expressed shock when she heard about my case, and I believe she relayed her concern to the Bundesamt. This provides the perfect explanation why the federal officer who denied my asylum was ashamed.

He wasn't alone in his mistake. Too often federal officers who determine refugee cases use the official language of the refugees' country of origin to determine their identity. This is wrong thinking and the case of the pregnant Togolese lady exemplifies this error. Not everyone in Africa speaks the country's official language. The vast majority are illiterate and don't even know what the official language of their country is.

Unlike Europe or North America, the countries of Africa don't have the simple luxury of one or two standard national languages spoken by the majority of the residents. For example, in a tiny country like Togo, which is only about four million in population, there are more than twenty different languages. Even neighbouring towns speak different dialects and people from one town do not understand the dialect of the other.

This language problem isn't limited to Africa. I met many East Indians, Bangladeshis and Pakistanis, who despite their countries being former colonies of the British Empire, did not speak English at all. Unfortunately, some of the officers who make these refugee decisions are entrenched in mistaken beliefs, so they make terrible decisions which they don't consider wrong.

A case in point was a fellow named Koffie whom I met at the refugee camp. Koffie claimed to be an Ivorian, but could not use his country to seek asylum because at that time it had no political problems. In his application for refugee status, he declared himself a Togolese citizen. The Federal Officer granted him an asylum claim because he spoke French, although he spoke not a single Togolese native language.

But I had something besides language and a pregnant woman to contend with daily – knife-wielding Kosovo Albanians and Bosnians refugees in this camp chasing me and any other black person. Whether it was at the canteen, telephone booth or the social service offices where we lined up to collect our pocket money or clothing, they always raised the tension level between themselves and us. They either jumped the queue or fixed a fellow countryman at the front, even though the fellow might have arrived late. When a protest occurred, they engaged in hurling threats and insults. You could ignore this behaviour when it happened once, but when it was done routinely with mischief, that was disrespect and something no one would tolerate.

This tension escalated whenever they saw one of their women talk to a black man. They didn't have the nerve to fight a black man one-on-on, so they armed themselves and attacked in groups. The authorities knew about their hostile and racist behaviour and tried to bunk them in separate buildings. It didn't always keep them away. Under cover of night, they snuck into our building and tried to strike as we slept. On numerous occasions they chased us from our buildings during the night, sometimes because one of them had experienced an altercation with a black man or they had seen a black man with an Albanian girl.

The Albanian men weren't the only danger. Their behaviour drew in the one sector I didn't want – the police. As soon as I saw a police car, I started worrying that the police had come to arrest me and get me deported. Then I had the added anxiety of finding a job to earn some money to pay my lawyer; otherwise he wouldn't render the services I needed. As all decisions from the Bundesamt or the court judge go through the lawyers, a refugee in arrears runs the risk of not receiving the Bundesamt or court decision, especially where an appeal must be made. And that could lead to arrest and deportation. So I prayed to be transferred and hoped to get away from that Godforsaken place.

Getting transferred could be complicated. In the questionnaire we filled out, we chose our transfer location. Refugees with relatives in other regions might want to be moved closer to their relatives. Usually their wishes were granted. However, they were exceptions. For the rest of us, the authorities had the last say.

Most refugees from this particular centre were normally transferred within the State of Bavaria's seventy-one *Landkreise* (administrative districts). Many claimants, though, preferred a transfer to the big cities for the obvious reasons, such as a better possibility of being issued the work permit compared to the restrictions smaller administrative districts place on refugee claimants.

Other factors included the actual prospect of obtaining a

good job and the fun of city living. Although German laws forbade refugees visiting other areas without a permit, which could be isolating for those living in a small town, a big city contained enough suburbs to move around in. For example, Neu Ulm, the city with the refugee transit centre where I first sought political asylum had a twin city called Ulm. This city is in the neighbouring state of Baden Württemberg while Neu Ulm is in the state of Bavaria. However, only the *Danube* River separates them and a boundary at the bridge connects the two cities. As a refugee claimant, I could not cross over to Ulm without obtaining a permit from the Bundesamt. The penalty if caught outside your administrative district without a permit was a fine or imprisonment.

So, instead of choosing my transfer destination, I decided to rely on luck. I guess the luck wasn't of the good variety, because after nearly four months at the camp, I was transferred to a very small town called Klein Koetz (Small Koetz) in Bavaria. This town was so small, the social workers who assisted refugees had never heard of it. Although it was less than twenty km from the refugee centre, they had to look it up on a map. I don't know if it would have made a difference if I had chosen a final destination in the questionnaire. In any case, I packed my bags and left for my new home. I felt relieved and happy just to get out of that Godforsaken camp, away from the daily racist taunts and abuse by Kosovo Albanians and living a life which always was on the line.

When I arrived in Klein Koetz it seemed as if I had returned home to Togo because I met about thirty black guys who hailed from there. To add to the coincidence, most of them were from my hometown of Sokode, the second largest city in Togo. There were also about twenty-five Kosovo Albanians, three Algerians, and an Egyptian. All of these were

Muslims. Despite my initial apprehension because of my experiences at the transit centre, those thirty black fellows filled me with some hope for survival because we outnumbered the Albanians. But as I would later find out, being in the majority didn't guarantee anything when it involved dealing with the Albanians.

We were living in a one-storey house, sharing a single telephone, a single kitchen, and a couple of washrooms. Unlike Canada or United States, Germany does not allow refugees to look for their own apartments. The government has homes called *Asyl Hiem* (Home for Refugees) scattered throughout the country and that is where they put refugees. These homes could be apartments or houses and depending on the size of the room, sometimes four, five, six, or seven people shared a room.

The disadvantage of being transferred to a small town soon began to show. I asked my colleagues about the general situation in the area and particularly about the job situation, because I needed money to pay my lawyer. Their answer gave me a shock. The authorities in the region did not issue work permit to refugee claimants.

Instead, they had a system called *Social Arbeit* (Social Work) and the authorities decided where refugees would work. The maximum pay for social work was two German marks per hour, which was about $1US at the time. This was far, far short of the minimum wage. The only incentive attached to doing social work was the authorities paid the cost of transportation to work. This effectively meant I made $8 for eight hours work, while my colleagues in the big cities made $8 per hour. The whole episode was modern-day slavery and as I found out, when I received my posting, the wage situation was more complicated and lopsided.

After a four-week wait, the authorities posted me to a

German senior citizens home, which was administered by the *Landratsamt Guenzburg.* (Guenzburg Regional Office). This seniors' home was a huge apartment complex with several other annexes. When I first arrived, my duties included cleaning the residence, mowing the lawn in summer and snow removal and salting during winter.

I discovered that some employers where the authorities sent my colleagues had kind hearts because they agreed to give them an extra $2.50, which brought their hourly rate to $3.50. At first the authorities wouldn't sanction the increase, but later they relented. But they ran into an inconsistency problem. How could they reconcile the fact that some refugees living at the same residence earned $3.50 per hour, while others made only $1 an hour? The simple solution should have been to raise everyone's pay to the same level.

Unfortunately, not every employer was sympathetic and reasonable. The authorities, i.e., the Guenzburg Regional Office, also didn't want the increase, because they figured that if refugees made more money it would only encourage more refugee claimants to pour into the country. We suggested that the authorities set up a rotational system to allow everyone a fair share of the cake. Negotiations were intense because some refugees who worked in the higher-paid areas didn't want to give up their privilege, even on a temporary basis. Finally, agreement was reached to allow us to swap our positions every month.

However, this monthly switch didn't work for me because the home's manager wanted me and no one else, so sent my replacement packing. When the authorities tried to explain the rational behind their decision, my manager stood her ground and offered to match the amount paid to my colleagues. That wouldn't do, the authorities said, and their word was law because the regional office directly controlled the seniors' home. The home and the authorities did reach a compromise – at the end of the month I received a fixed amount, but it was much lower than my friends' earnings. But I accepted it because I had the luxury of staying at one place and not being moved around arbitrarily.

The low wages didn't stop me from doing an honest day's work and doing it efficiently. Besides wanting to hang on to me for life, my employer also showed appreciation by appointing me assistant caretaker of the complex and its annexes. My responsibilities included painting the apartment buildings and rooms of deceased seniors to make way for newcomers. I also continued to plow the snow and mow the lawn, as well as water the flowers, prune the trees and shrubs, and do electrical work and general maintenance.

I proved so resourceful to them that I scared other workers away. When I first started, the government had contracted a company to paint the entire complex and my employers asked me to assist where necessary. However, two days after the company had started painting, I arrived at work to find the company workers packing their equipment.

"What's going on?" I asked.

"The authorities want you to do all the work," they said as they loaded their supplies into their van.

My employer confirmed this change-of-work plan. For nearly a year I got the job done, painting the interior of the huge buildings during winter and the exterior during the summer. I saved the government thousands of dollars because they paid me less than the *Landratsamt* paid professional painters.

Both the *Landratsamt* and my boss at the seniors' home were so pleased with my capabilities and trusted my integrity so much that they didn't bring in any replacement during my boss's vacation or absence. I never had any vacation myself because of my status and the meagre pay I was receiving.

Some people might not consider a caretaker's job as a big deal, but for me as a Black African and a refugee in Bavaria, Germany, it was a big deal. So, despite the low pay and the shenanigans of the authorities that kept me there, I enjoyed doing the work. I liked the responsibilities. I also felt proud that I was helping the most vulnerable and helpless in society.

Despite my responsibilities and my boss's appreciation, there was another administrative oddity. During the nearly three years (May 1996 to February 1999) that I worked here for the authorities, they still maintained in my files that I was *arbeitloss* (jobless) throughout my entire stay in the country. The kicker was the addendum – they listed me as a social assistance recipient.

FIVE

Germany – Foreigner Bashing and Auslander Politik

Election time in Bavaria is a scary experience for a foreigner. The manifesto is xenophobic and highly inflammatory. Flyers and signs scream *Auslander Raus* (Foreigners Out) or *Auslander Kriminalitat* (Criminal Foreigners), referring to all aliens as criminals. Foreigners have always been blamed and made scapegoats for anything from drug trafficking to impregnating German girls, some of which is true, but the ferocity at which it's often portrayed is way out of proportion.

These anti-refugee feelings are exacerbated because of the claims that refugees are just economic migrants who are in the country only to take advantage of the generous German social and healthcare system at the taxpayers' expense. However, the politicians don't tell the citizens about situations like mine, which was more or less modern-day slavery.

It must be noted that *Bayern* (Bavaria) by far is the most conservative state in the former West Germany, if not the entire German Federation. Bavaria is so conservative that it has its own political party, The Christian Socialist Union or CSU, which does not seek elections in other German states, and which has ruled Bavaria uninterrupted for almost fifty years. It's sister party happened to be one of the two main political parties in Germany, the centre right Christian Democratic Union, CDU, the party of the legendary German ex-chancellor, Helmet Kohl. The other main party, of course, is the centre left Social Democratic Party, SDP.

The CSU is a far right party even though its leaders and supporters don't want to admit it. This party is so extreme that politicians in this particular region have often used anti-foreigner, anti-refugee rhetoric to resonate with the public so they vote them into power. For example, the Bavarian firebrand, Premier Edmund Stoiber, who almost won the federal election during the country's leadership elections in 2003, has gained notoriety by making inflammatory statements, mainly against foreigners.

These foreigners include the large Turkish population in the country, who were brought in as guest workers to help rebuild Germany after the devastation of the Second World War. Stoiber is so extreme and xenophobic, he once supported fellow populist and rightwing extremist, Austrian Politician Georg Hader, when the latter was under fire from the international community for racist and anti-immigrant comments he had made during an Austrian election campaign. And Stoiber's predecessor, Josef Strauss, was so anti-foreigner that gossip has it that he once offered to pay, out of his own pocket, the entire cost to deport all refugee claimants in Bavaria.

When faced with actually living in this hostile anti-foreigner environment, I began to wonder why I asked for political asylum in that particular state. Back home in Africa, I used to watch the *Bundes Liga* (German soccer league) broadcast on GBC, the Ghanaian government-owned TV station. The Bavarian soccer team, *Bayern Munchen*, was my favourite German club. I was such a fanatic supporter of the team, it never occurred to me to look at the politics of that state.

The hostilities were so bad that they sometimes became almost physical and fatal. On several occasions my colleagues and I had close calls and were at the risk of being run over by automobiles. As I thumbed my way along a road, trying to get a ride, the scenario usually went like this:

The driver blew his car's horn and pulled over. I raced to the automobile.

"Can you give me a ride to Guenzburg?" I smiled at him.

The driver slid down the window of the car and scowled at me.

"Was machts du in Deutschland Schwarzenegger?" he asked. Then he hit the accelerator and shoved off onto the road. He then stuck a hand out the open window and gave me the finger.

And the scenario repeated itself because to get to my refugee home, I had to walk along this road. And I had to take this road because Sunday and holiday train schedules to the station fifty meters from my home didn't jive with my work schedule. So I had to catch the bus at the nearest major intersection, one kilometer along this road. I was a major target on this road.

Going to the police wasn't the answer because they also had their own form of racism against us. My colleagues and I were fed up with it and one Friday afternoon, the antagonism came to a head.

My friends and I had finished work and as usual, we sat at the station waiting for the train to take us home to our town, twenty kilometers away. Two police officers, a male and a female approached us

"Ausweise Bitte?" ("IDs please?") They asked.

They'd done this routine so many times before and gotten away with it, but today, my friends and I acted spontaneously and simultaneously. We kept our IDs in our pockets and stared at them. How dare they always pick on us even though they didn't bother other non-German citizens waiting for the train? How dare they hit on us because of our skin color?

"What you're doing is pure racism," one of my friends said.

"Neo-Nazi's," another friend muttered under his breath, but the police officers missed that one. Just as well because that could have landed us in very serious trouble, with serious consequences that none of us could predict.

In today's Germany, it is illegal to call someone a Nazi. No question, there are extreme right-wing hooligans, skinheads and rednecks who label themselves Neo-Nazis with pride. But most of the population sees these people as a disenchanted bunch of hopeless fanatics and bigots who are out of touch with reality. To a great many Germans, the word "Nazi" is taboo, and they consider it insulting and very offensive when the outside world refers to modern-day Germans as Nazis. They believe a lot is changed in Germany since 1945 and think the world should move on.

So, it was in this context that our little confrontation with the police occurred.

"Give me your ID." The male officer glowered at us, while his partner snarled.

In a show of force, the duo began detaching their handcuffs from their uniforms. But we stood and stared back at them.

"Come on boys, let's see some co-operation," the male officer said.

"Yeah, boys," his partner repeated. "Come on. We're only doing our jobs. Show us your IDs and you can be on your way."

"Yeah?" I asked. "Does that job include racial profiling? We're not the only people at the station. We'll show you our IDs after you've checked everyone else here."

"No, you'll show your IDs right now," the female officer

said and grabbed the front of my friend's shirt.

"Right now! That's an order or you're under arrest," her partner said, dangling his handcuffs."

Now all eyes at the station focused on our confrontation and something surprising happened. One group at the end of the station moved forward and one of them said, "Hey officer, wait a moment. They have a point."

"Yeah," some of the others said.

They moved closer to us and seemed to form a half circle around the police, but it wasn't a friendly circle of protection. The two police officers shrugged their shoulders and stepped over to the group.

"IDs, please," they said, and didn't stop until they checked the ID of everyone – black and white.

We had won a small but significant victory. Not only did we manage to ensure our dignity as human beings, but after that day, the police hesitated to do on-the-spot ID checks on us. And some of my friends milked this uneven truce for all they could. They randomly stopped the police in their cruisers and asked for a ride or directions even when they didn't need them.

In any area of society, not everyone is a bad nut. In retrospect, my life in the small town was not all that bleak. After months of isolation and anxiety, I began making friends. Amidst the skinheads were some beautiful German ladies.

To me they were angels who made me proud and also made me feel like a human being. I probably met too many of them, but I also met individuals who were high profile from my perspective as a refugee and a black man. In an unexpected twist, the senior visa officer at the regional headquarters of the Foreign Office became a personal friend and helped me in so many ways. On several occasions during my early days at the refugee home, she took me to work in her own private car.

She just called me one evening and said I could skip taking the social assistance branch van to work. She was going to drive me. My friends were agog, and when they saw how well the visa officer and I got along, they thought I could have a go with her. But that was not what I wanted. I was happy to have a special relationship with a person in her position and I was willing to keep it that way.

For a few months, the officer continued to come from her home in Gross Koetz (Bigger Koetz) to my refugee home in its twin town, Klein Koetz and drive me to work. After all I was on the only route to her office in the capital. Then it stopped. I considered the interference here as racially related and caused by the other passenger in the car – a young German lady who also lived in Gross Koetz and worked in the same office as the visa officer.

From the very first day I had the feeling the young lady was not happy riding in the same car as a black man. I could feel my presence was a nightmare for her. She had shown that by her actions and attitude over and over again. She was initially very mean and snobbish, but later I began to think she might have been jealous of my friendship with the senior officer.

When she came up with a plan, I figured it was a cynical ploy to get rid of me. By this time the van had stopped picking up my colleagues and they were taking the train to work. Her plan called for me to also use the train. She would make sure the government paid for my monthly pass because that was one of her job functions. She used the reasoning that as I started work one hour later than her and the visa officer, I lost an hour's sleep for a ride.

But I didn't find getting up early a problem. Doing what the visa officer said – this woman issued visas and had authority to refuse their renewal which could result in immediate deportation – was more than any inconvenience I suffered. Despite the change of events, the senior officer continued to help me on several fronts for the next three years. The biggest surprise was the younger lady and I eventually became good friends, too.

I also began falling in love with cute and sweet German girls – blondes, with blue eyes, green eyes, you name it, which sometimes made me forgot my problems and all that racist garbage that was going on. For two years, work and sleep were the only orders of my day. Hearing about all the fun, financial success and love from my friends in Munich, Augsburg and Stuggart didn't help. Although I thought they embellished most of their stories, I began to feel I was missing out on real living.

My big break into the world of fun soon arrived when some of my friends went to a club in Guenzburg, the district capital. When they returned they couldn't stop talking about all the beautiful babes they'd encountered and the wonderful reception they had. I cursed myself and wondered what the hell I was doing – after all I wasn't a monk or a slave. I decided to go to the club the following week. The place was a blast.

For the next three weeks I saw different babes at the club. There were at least five whom I reckoned were in love with me. Making a choice became very difficult, although I favoured the one nicknamed Melanie. She was without a question my heart's desire. But she was so beautiful and so popular at the club I felt I didn't stand a chance. I felt inferior. Weak in the presence of beauty, some might say. I was shy and intimidated to talk with her even though it was obvious she always wanted to talk to me.

Another reason I hesitated from making a move was the guy constantly in her company. He was her fellow – blond, blue eyed, well-dressed – who always arrived at the club in a different posh car. The two were very popular and appeared to be perfectly matched. They danced together, especially when slow German music was played. But every time we left the club, my friends asked me, "What's wrong? That lady is madly in love with you. Are you too timid to take your chances?"

They couldn't persuade me. I couldn't imagine myself, a black man and a poor refugee, without even a bicycle competing with that gentleman. As I dithered about what to do with Melanie, one of my colleagues hit on her. Melanie told him to back off or face severe consequences. That warning started the ball rolling for me.

I now knew that my fears had legs. Melanie didn't want me so I decided to make a move on the other ladies. One by one, I made love to them. However, one thing I observed with German girls was that if you made good love to them, they didn't keep it a secret. They blabbed about it to their girlfriends who had not yet had a go with me.

Meantime, when the word got out, Melanie started acting jealous and turned aggressive. As one of the club's waitresses she was at huge disadvantage. In between taking and delivering food and drink orders, it was difficult for her to have any meaningful conversation with me. So, she began to follow me outside to see what I was up to with the other ladies.

One day when she saw me in the thick of affairs with another lady, she broke. She stomped back into the club. I could hear her complain to her best friend, Karin, who also baby sat her daughter. When I re-entered the club, Karin came at me.

"Ali, you stupid, boy, you're making Melanie upset."

"What the…?" I scratched my head. What was going on? Melanie and I were friends but there'd never been talk of any romantic relationship. And I was still too nervous to talk to her about love. I felt very sad and confused.

I shrugged my shoulders at Karin and walked over to Tony, the DJ, and sat beside him. Tony often invited me to do stand-in as MC and that made me even more popular at the club. My friends realizing I wasn't dancing as I used to, came over.

"What's wrong with you?" they asked.

I shrugged my shoulders. Then Karin walked up to me. What now, I wondered.

"Melanie's asked me to take you to her apartment when the club closes. She'll follow later after she finishes up at the club."

At 3 a.m., Karin took me to Melanie's apartment. Thirty minutes later Melanie arrived home. By then I had already taken my shower and had gone straight to bed and waited for whatever she had in store for me. As I expected, she also took her shower and then came over and lay beside me on the bed. She took my hands. I concluded it was now or never. I cautiously moved my hands around her two gorgeous breasts. We then came face to face and as soon as our mouths met, we started intense kissing.

I moved my mouth to her breasts and started kissing and sucking them one after the other. At that point, it was obvious she lost control of herself. At the same time, my left middle finger was busy working hard in her private part. I continued to operate on her body for a while. As her body continued to weaken and her orgasm became extremely high, I moved towards the lower part of her body and without any delay, penetrated her private part. She let out a loud scream.

She continued to scream all morning as I continued to move up and down, side by side and making the occasional deeper penetration inside her private part. She screamed so loud and for such a long period of time that her friend and her husband, who was my fellow refugee, got angry and complained bitterly about it. After two hours of what was perhaps the best lovemaking I ever had, we fell asleep. We didn't wake up until 9 a.m. What a day that was and what a dream come true. Later she told me the guy I had feared was gay.

I breathed a sigh of relief.

SIX

Germany - Jealous and Racist Albanians

As I began to enjoy life with my newfound love and beauty queen, racism stuck its ugly nose into our affair. The threats barrelled in from all fronts – friends, family and foes. Melanie's friends and relatives threatened to shun her if she continued her relationship with what they called *Schwarzenegger* (Black Nigger).

The Kosovo Albanians at my refugee residence, who were already jealous about any black guy who made love to a white girl, decided to up the ante in perpetuating racial tension. They considered themselves white and superior to us and it bothered them that we had women falling at our feet at the clubs, while they were left standing alone at the same clubs. It never occurred to them that the ladies avoided them because they didn't like their aggressive behaviour – threatening with knives and sticks, violently banging on the doors of the washrooms trying to force others using it to come out, firing noisy pellet guns, screaming, yelling and beating up their girlfriends. So, the Kosovo Albanians decided to vent their frustration on me in particular.

A few days after Melanie and I first made love at her apartment, she decided to visit me at my refugee home. I knew the Kosovo Albanians liked to hover outside my door and listen whenever I had a female visitor. So I prepared by upping my stereo system to full blare to muffle any noise Melanie might make as that was her trademark in lovemaking.

So Melanie arrived and we were just getting started when everything ceased – music, lights and us. I got up to investigate, pushed passed the Albanians outside the door and found they had removed the fuses at the main electrical panel, leaving the whole house in silent darkness. They had only done it to ease their eavesdropping so they had ammunition to complain to the authorities about the inconveniences I supposedly caused them.

The following morning, their banging on my door woke me. Melanie had left by 3 a.m. but they still complained that I was not letting them sleep and began threatening me. But something else was happening simultaneously in the residence. The authorities had started sending most of my countrymen back home while the Albanians were doubling their numbers. Their former Yugoslavia was embroiled in civil strife. The former Serbian President, Slobodan Milosevic, was sending his troops to kill the Kosovo Albanians and the latter fled for their life to Germany, many to Klein Koetz and to my residence. So the balance of power in my residence had shifted dramatically to the Albanians.

They couldn't be deported to their homeland, Kosovo, so they had nothing to lose by turning bolder with their harassment against us blacks. One evening, though, they took it to another level. I had a phone call and went to the residence's only phone. As soon as I picked it up, three of them showed up and started marching by me – two in one direction and the other in the opposite direction. This third fellow turned around and stomped back to me.

"Get off phone. Get off phone." His voice rose with each word.

I covered one ear and tried to get on with my call.

"Get off phone. I need to call home. I need to call Pristina."

"Excuse me," I said into the phone's receiver and looked over at the guy.

"Okay. Just give me a few minutes to finish my call and you can have the phone."

"No, no, no. You have to get off phone now. I need to call Pristina. Get off phone now." He started jumping around.

I heard sounds like an army and saw his friends coming towards me from all sides, those from downstairs, and from the east and west wings of our building. I was outnumbered and didn't want to do anything stupid.

"Why are you acting like this?" I asked the first guy.

All of a sudden the smallest, but most temperamental of them, grabbed me by the throat and squeezed me to the wall. I pushed him off me, and as he fell to the floor, some of the others joined in while some ran away, probably for the knives and sticks, which they were noted for. Before they returned, I managed to free myself and made my way downstairs and outside the building. When I turned back, I saw that some of my African brothers had already escaped through the windows; some jumped from the top floor.

I was disappointed that my African colleagues didn't come to my defence, but I wasn't surprised. The Kosovo Albanians' history of stabbing and killing Africans at several refugee homes throughout Germany might have scared my friends. Here, where I lived, the situation was no different. They raised the tempo and tension with the use of the washrooms, the kitchen and other amenities. They hogged the only telephone in the residence, yet tried to prevent us from a few minutes talking time. To avoid confrontation, my colleagues and I usually trekked to a telephone booth about a kilometer away.

They also deflated the tires on our girlfriends' cars and called our girlfriends "prostitutes." They provided some humour because they had the twisted notion that the German girls loved us because black people are said to have a much bigger penis. When our girlfriends visited, the Albanians paraded out in their underwear, in an attempt to show the girls they had big genitals. Sometimes they coached each other about how to catch our women's attention.

They continued their confrontational and racist manoeuvres at the foreign office where we renewed our visa. One of their tactics was to harass us for our bathing habits. They should talk. They went for days without bathing except for quick face and hair washes. And they smelled. We washed twice or more a day, but they claimed that the only reason we bathed regularly was because we wanted to wash our dirty black skin so we could become white like them.

So, for today's episode, while my African friends didn't help, Melanie, who was on the other end of the phone line, did. She could hear the yelling in the background. When the call ended abruptly, she must have realized something was amiss and called her girlfriend. As I stood outside, Melanie's girlfriend, who lived a few kilometers from my residence, ran up to me. I told her what had happened.

"Call the police," she said. She pulled out her cell phone and started to dial 110, the German version of 911, but I stopped her because I figured they could become more dangerous if any of them were arrested.

"But you can't just do nothing," she said. "Look I'll write a report about the incident and you can send it to the regional foreign office.

She did and I did the following day. When the senior visa official heard the news, she became angry but she was not surprised because the Albanians had gained notoriety throughout Germany for stabbing to death black refugees at various refugee homes. For that reason she decided to transfer me to another town.

I agreed to go until I heard the proposed new place also had Kosovo Albanians. I felt it wouldn't have made any difference and I did not want to give the Kosovo Albanians any reason to believe they had forced me out. Threats of violence weren't going to intimidate me. I told the visa official I wanted to stay. Both she and my girlfriend tried to persuade me otherwise, but I was determined to hang in here. In short I did not want to be intimidated by threats of violence, so I told her I wanted to stay. Melanie, fearing for my life, bought me a pepper spray.

And so the war of nerves continued. A few days after this confrontation, some of the Albanians urinated and threw dairy waste on my doorstep. I didn't want to accost them every time they did something stupid, so I kept silent and cleaned it up. Several months later I was the sole black man left in the residence. Most of my colleagues had either been deported or fled to nearby countries to avoid deportation.

This time the Albanians were not at fault. The culprit was who I thought to be a narrow-minded racist individual named Stefan, one of the few "bad apple" Germans. Stefan had been transferred from the Neu Ulm refugee transit centre when it closed a few months earlier. His new destination was the Guenzburg Administrative District, which falls under the jurisdiction of Augsburg, the regional headquarters of the area where I lived. This fellow who seemed to me to hate blacks became the number one enemy of my colleagues.

However, I was more determined than ever to stick it out. I

was always on the alert, be it in my room, the kitchen or the washroom. I felt stronger than ever in my resilience and resolve towards the Albanians. The police presence also became frequent, and that caused them to stop and think first. And their thoughts, although imaginative, helped me. They believed that I was an informer for the authorities, probably derived from my relationship with some individuals at the foreign office. They also thought I was armed with a shotgun. Some of them now wanted to reconcile with me.

The point, though, was whatever side you took with these fellows, they never changed. If you questioned something they did, they turned confrontational and threatened violence even when caught in the act. So, you could imagine what they might do if I suddenly wanted to become their new best friend.

And yet logic should put me in line to be their friend. I was one of the staunchest critics of their number one enemy, the former Yugoslav President Milosevic who was persecuting them and the Bosnian Muslims. Despite the slaughter in their homeland, they hung onto their twisted beliefs, namely that their situation was no worse than that occurring in Africa and that they were superior to black people. Some, if not all of them added a third belief – they considered the massacres and brutalities going on in their homeland as a good thing, because they figured it helped their cause to be recognized as refugees.

Not content with phone shenanigans, they turned to bicycle thievery, stealing our bicycle parts or the whole bicycle. On numerous occasions they deflated the tires of Julia, a friend of mine and also of Melanie. Julia came from the city of Donauwouth, the capital of *Landkreise* Donauwouth. After Melanie and I broke up, Julia was in the picture more. The Albanians stole a brand new bicycle Julia had bought me so I could ride with her on her vacation to Ingolstadt, the home of the Audi. Her employers had planned the riding trip for the company's employees and everyone was urged to make the trip with their partner.

Unfortunately, because of the Albanians' actions, I was forced to use an old bicycle which caused me a lot of problems. The rusty chain kept coming out and the paddling was extremely difficult during our forty kilometer trip. On many occasions, the lead group had to stop and wait for us. Other times, they gave up and left us behind.

The Albanians also refused to do the social work we did. Instead they did "black jobs," work done under the table. They could do this because of "skin color," i.e., while they considered themselves whites and European, many, such as the Serbs, in Europe saw them as the by-product of Turkish invaders. It was easy for them to cross into Germany without having to board an airplane.

It was also a common fact that authorities accepted their asylum applications ninety percent more often than they did for Black Africans because the Albanian plight was always in the spotlight. The bottom line was the police knew most Albanians had residence or work permits as opposed to the small number of black residents. It was like separating rice from beans.

Meanwhile, my overall situation began going downhill. As hinted above, my relationship with Melanie had hit a snag because of the continuous pressure from somc anti-black elements in her camp. The situation became so serious we were unable to visit each other, so we resorted to going out of town to make love, including going into the forests. As part of our troubles, a Gambian friend, Gaye, who had given us access to his apartment, tried to seduce Melanie.

Melanie was in a conundrum. Events became so bizarre; Melanie was finally forced to send me a letter. "In broken English." She wrote, in part:

Hi Sweetie

Babe I must tell you something that makes you very, very sad. But I don't want to play with you and your feelings. You don't deserve to be given a lie. I must be honest to you. So, I write a letter because I am cowardly to tell you these things to your face.

I want to break our relationship.

I have a big problem with the meanings of my friends. They are very important for me and I cannot say that they are care for me.

I like you very much and the time with you was very, very nice, but it is not enough for me to stay by you forever.

Now, before our relationship is very deep and your feelings for me are very high, I break this.

Please Ali, try to understand me a little bit and don't get very angry with me. Maybe we can have a friendship if you still have to come to terms with the disappointment.

Sorry, Babe.

I was devastated. Melanie was the best love I ever had at the time. She made me proud. She made me feel like I was sitting on top of the world. Even the hostile Albanians admitted I had hit a jackpot by having her. Melanie was beautiful both inside and outside, and for me as a refugee to lose such a fine human being tore at my heart and soul.

SEVEN

ONE MAN'S CRUSADE

But my problems didn't stop there. Of course, I had the ongoing situations with the paranoid Kosovo Albanians. Then Stefan, the anti-black official at the Foreign office, sent me a letter

Dear Ali: *November, 1998*

You are hereby advised to appear at room 313 at the foreign office in Landratsamt Guenzburg to sign a document for your voluntary repatriation. It is important you make this appearance on the date and room mentioned above, failure of which could result in your immediate arrest, detention and deportation.

Sincerely Yours
Stefan.

I knew Stefan when he was still at the refugee reception centre at Neu Ulm. His stone face and lanky build made a lie of the axiom "don't judge a book by its cover." Stefan had gained notoriety with refugees because of his seemingly racist behaviour and other extraordinary measures.

Before Stefan's arrival at the regional office, the authorities used to ask refugee claimants to go to their various embassies to get their own travel documents. When I first saw him, his responsibility was to pay social assistance to refugee claimants. This put him front and centre daily with refugees. He hated to pay them. He appeared to resent any foreigner, whether colored or not.

His office opened from 9 a.m. to 12 p.m. noon, but he always arrived a little late. By that time, hundreds of refugees packed the foyer of his office. When he arrived, he glared at us, unlocked his office door, went inside and hid. Thirty minutes later, he unlocked his door and we all lined up, hoping that he was at last ready to serve us.

"You better all behave yourselves if you want me to help you." Stefan slid the door partially open and stuck his head out, but made no move to open the door all the way.

"Ah," we said.

"We've been waiting since 7 a.m.," the fellow twentieth in line said.

"Quiet," Stefan said. "Or I won't serve you at all."

He closed the door and went over to the sideboard and boiled some water. Then he made tea and sat down at his desk. He leaned back in his chair, made a show of sipping tea, muttering "Ah," and stared out the window. He repeated this a few times, then made a few phone calls. Half an hour later, he stood up, walked to the door and opened it.

"Okay, you." He pointed to the first fellow in line. Come in here for your money."

He continued at this deliberate leisurely pace until his short time, reduced to two hours or less, was up. He served about a dozen of us.

And so went his daily routine, with his behaviour and attitude definitely upping the tension ante every day. Some individuals had to wait days to claim their money because of their shifting position in the line-up – one day they might be near the front of the queue and just miss getting served, the next day they could be at the back.

So, when I went to the foreign office in Guenzburg and saw him there for the first time, I told my friends about him, but they shrugged me off. Most of them were transferred to our residence via other refugee transit centers; in effect they did not encounter him and hence their skepticism about my warnings.

In any case, there he now was, posted to the office of Frau Becker who was in charge of deporting refugees whose claims for refugee status had been turned down. From the word "go," it was like this guy was on a mission, a mission to rid the Guenzburg district of black people. Within a month of his arrival, he had started on his crusade using several tactics.

Every time my friends and I showed up to renew our visa, he'd open his office door, and when he saw us he'd walk over to the visa office and act as if he were in charge, yelling instructions to the two officers there, including one Frau Gehle, who was supposed to be the supervisor, but she cowered in front of him. Before he arrived, our visas were renewed for two to three months, but Stefan changed that to as little as five days or less. We also discovered he usually come in to the visa office only when Frau Gehle, the timid one, was around, because she was the only one who asked him how many days for our visa renewal.

Stefan's antics didn't stop there. He reversed what had evolved into almost an anomaly in this district – the authorities and claimants had mutual respect and understanding. No refugee had ever been forcefully deported or even taken by authorities to their own embassies to secure travel documents. The latter put the refugees at greater risk because by showing up there with officials, they could be deported to a country where they feared persecution.

Instead, authorities usually let claimants voluntarily go on their own to their respective embassies in Bonn and arrange to get their own travel documents. Of course, in most cases, they were refused. But it gave claimants some breathing space and prolonged their stay, which eventually led to their being granted temporary or permanent residency.

Stefan, however, brought the policies of the refugee reception centre with him. He forgot or ignored that these centers screened claimants to weed out the criminal elements and anyone with a record was deported immediately. Here, in these regional offices, refugees had already been screened and were contributing to the economy of the region and country.

In just under a year, Stefan had chalked up quite a track record. He had single-handedly forced over thirty black refugees out of the region. He sent us all letters that we would be taken to Bonn to pick up our travel documents for deportation. A couple of black refugees left voluntarily, and the others escaped to neighbouring states.

Stefan's reputation continued to grow, almost causing the death of my colleague, Ghazi. Earlier Stefan had sent Ghazi notice to prepare for his repatriation. But for some reason, one day, Stefan sent the police to forcefully arrest him. Ghazi had told us plainly he was willing to return home, voluntarily. He asked only for a few more weeks to make his final preparation. When the police banged on his door and he realized he wasn't going to be allowed to leave voluntarily, he jumped out a first floor window of our building. He then hid in a nearby forest.

But it was winter, with snow everywhere and the temperature was below freezing. Even more disturbing, he wasn't a healthy person. He had crooked legs so he couldn't walk like a normal person. Within a matter of minutes he came out of his hiding place and Stefan and the police arrested him and subsequently deported him. There was no question that Ghazi's actions were suicidal and stupid, but the incident showed to me how brutal Stefan was in his mission.

It was now November 1998 and I was the only black refugee left in the home. My letter about my trip to Bonn (the former German capital) finally arrived. I wasn't surprised – I'd been expecting it. I knew that he was the one who had instigated the second rejection of my refugee claim. As my second refugee claim had taken me close to a year, nine months longer than most second applications, it seemed that my claim would be granted. Until Stefan arrived and applied pressure. My asylum request was rejected.

The rejection letter itself, however, was written in a moderate and subdued tone. This time the authorities accepted the crucial issue of my identity and nationality. The letter further stated that the only reason my claim had been rejected was because there were no more political persecutions or other problems in my country; therefore, I could safely return home.

I did not want to go to my country's Embassy. Embassies represent governments in other countries. Therefore, a refugee claimant who is taken to his or her country's embassy technically becomes a refugee if he or she wasn't already one. This is because, among other things, the claimant is forced to give detailed personal information which the government may not have before, thus exposing the claimant to further danger. It is important to mention that in the majority of cases, political asylum seekers are people fleeing dictatorships and these dictators don't see anything good about their nationals seeking political asylum.

There have been countless examples where claimants have been returned to their country and then disappeared upon arrival, despite assurances from the dictators to the deporting governments that the claimants will not be harmed. Governments deporting refugee claimants knows it is illegal; that is why when they take a claimant to an embassy, they tell the embassy officials the person is an illegal immigrant.

So, going to my Embassy would expose me to further danger because my country's authorities would now have more information about me especially that I had lived in Ghana for a long time. And that wasn't good because Ghana is the country the Togo regime accused of backing Togolese dissidents plotting to overthrow it. Of course, there were numerous cases where refugees were returned under the same circumstances. I didn't want their fate –disappearance or death.

However, I had only two choices, either to go with Stefan voluntarily or face arrest and forced deportation. The decision was a tough one to make. Finally, I relented and I agreed to go with him to the Embassy in Bonn. One side of me hoped that he might have a change of heart and abort his plans to send me there. But the other side of me remembered that this guy was on a mission and nothing could stop him.

I managed to thwart one of Stefan's plans that we travel to Bonn in a police car, but not without a fight. I told my lawyer I wasn't a criminal and no way was I going to ride in a police van. Stefan, however, made excuses to my lawyer – they knew I wasn't a criminal, but they were taking a violent incarcerated criminal to Bonn for his travel documents and it was simpler and cheaper for us all to go in a police van. My lawyer caved and advised me to agree, but I refused and stood my ground. Eventually the authorities gave in and in November 1998, I traveled with Stefan to Bonn in a car provided by the regional office.

Usually refugees went into hiding and escape as soon as they received notification to be repatriated because they feared authorities might pick them up at any time. I decided to stay on to see things through. Although I didn't know the exact date when I would qualify to make another asylum application, I did know I could do so after three years. That time was coming closer before Stefan wrote me.

I hoped that my situation would drag on for another couple of months. Stefan, though, was bent on going to Bonn with me. After he had made his arrangements, he informed me, he would pick me up at my refugee home between 3 and 4 a.m. True to his promise, Stefan and another officer, who was to be our driver arrived on schedule. We left early because of the distance. Koetz to Bonn was about 350 km. We had to drive through heavy snow and had to arrive at the Togolese Embassy before it closed.

Stefan had already arranged with a representative of the International Organization for Migration (IOM) to meet us at the Embassy. The IOM purchases tickets for refugees and prepares their repatriation. Their policy is to assist governments to repatriate refugees, who wish to return home voluntarily, not those refugees which governments are deporting. Governments are responsible for the cost of deporting refugees. The IOM representative appeared at the embassy, but shouldn't have been there because my arriving with Stefan meant I wasn't a willing returnee. However, because some governments are the main source of IOM budgets, the IOM sometimes helps governments engaged in clandestine operations.

And Stefan was engaged in one with me. He couldn't afford missing that day because; a reservation had already been booked by the IOM on a KLM flight. Therefore, failure to get confirmation that I would obtain a travel document that day meant postponement – exactly what I was looking for.

So, on that snowy November day, Stefan, the other officer

and I started our journey to Bonn. Driving conditions were terrible, especially for a trip over 300 kilometers. It didn't help that neither Stefan nor the driver knew the route. Stefan had a map and was directing the driver, and we seemed to be making our way steadily from city to city. On two occasions we lost our way. But the most serious occurred when we had rejoined a highway near the city of Frankfurt after we have exited to urinate. We discovered we were headed in the opposite direction.

Several kilometers later we were able to exit and rejoined our main highway to Bonn. This was all amid the dangerous weather and driving conditions. All those impeding factors worked to my benefit and I wanted more so that we didn't reach Bonn. I prayed for our car to stall or a minor accident to occur. When you are a refugee who doesn't want to return home, you think crazy thoughts and schemes.

Meanwhile, Stefan showed me his human side and attempted to put ice on his otherwise rigid policies. Throughout the journey, he tried to be friendly, and wanted me to believe that he was just obeying orders. On two occasions en route to Bonn, he asked the driver to stop so that we could eat some breakfast and lunch. I told him, I didn't have money but he said he would take care of that.

At about 2 p.m. local time, we arrived in Bonn. So much for my wish list. We went straight to the Togolese Embassy, where the IOM representative waited.

Also at the embassy were a few fellow refugees, there to secure travel documents. I sat down with them and we exchanged stories. Stefan didn't appreciate this, so he pulled me aside and gave me two orders: don't tell anyone why I am here and don't tell the embassy officials I am a refugee.

I gathered from my friends that they came on their own and were trying to fix their future by paying money to the embassy staff so that the latter wouldn't prepare the travel documents. No travel documents meant no deportation or repatriation. When it was my turn, I went in for my interview. The officials told me that the document would be mailed to officials at my regional office.

The surprise of the day happened on our way back home. As we approached the city of Stuggart, Stefan asked the driver to exit the highway. We drove straight to a luxurious restaurant. After getting us seated, Stefan got us water and some pop. He told me to order anything I wanted to eat. Again, I told him I didn't have money, but again he told me not to worry and that he would take care of everything.

We made it to my refugee home in Koetz at about 7:30 p.m. where they dropped me off.

I decided to spend less time at the refugee home. In some administrative regions, especially in Augsburg, the authorities had the habit of picking up refugee claimants in the middle of the night for deportation, despite their having signed documents to voluntarily return to their home countries.

In this situation, the only belongings the claimant can bring are the clothes on their back. By law, officials can remove claimants by force only when they refuse to sign documents to return home voluntarily. The authorities do their snatching in wee hours so that refugees cannot contact their lawyer.

I stayed with Francis, a Ghanaian guy whom I'd befriended a few months earlier. Francis lived in Donauwouth, about 60 km from Koetz. To avoid any suspicion that I wasn't going to escape, I continued with my work at the seniors' home and kept my room at the refugee home.

Each day I went to work and then stopped at the refugee home to check my mail and then traveled to Francis' place to pass the night. Checking my mail was very important because after the Bonn visit, there was the possibility the foreign office would write me once they received my travel documents. Notice to report to them could come at any time and if I failed to do so, that could mean immediate arrest and deportation. I was doing everything to avoid that.

I wasn't particularly comfortable staying at Francis' place because I discovered he was a chain smoker of weed. I'd never smoked even a cigarette in my life, let alone marijuana, so it was a bit hard for me, but I wasn't looking for luxury. And Francis' German ex-wife, Ramona, was also a drug addict, despite supposedly just completing her rehabilitation treatment for drugs. When I arrived she was out on probation.

Francis and Ramona maintained a strange relationship for a divorced couple. They had an ironclad bond so strong that Francis was able to convince Ramona to get a clip of her son's hair to give to a drug addict he knew who had to provide a hair sample to the police.

Even stranger, perhaps, was my growing relationship with Ramona. Despite her drug problems, I found her to be a very good loving woman. Our relationship became so tight she shocked me one Saturday evening. It was about 6 p.m. when Francis' phone rang. He picked it up, said Ramona wanted to speak to me and handed the receiver to me.

"I'm going to surprise you," Ramona said. She sounded very happy. "I'm going to have you make love to a very beautiful German blonde. She's a 20 year old good friend of mine."

"Where are you?" I asked.

"Oh, in a nearby town. I can get to your place at about 8 p.m. I have Francis' car and I promised to pick my friend up at the train station. Then I'll come by and pick you and Francis up and we can all go have fun at my place."

True to her word, Ramona and her friend arrived just after 8 p.m. to pick up Francis and me. Ramona made an indirect reference to my new beauty queen, Suzy, and then got into a heavy argument with Francis. I kept mute through all this, so didn't say a word to Suzy until we arrived at Ramona's place and were more formally introduced.

The original plan was for us all to go to a club, but Suzy and I entered into some tense romance hours after the introduction, and it was impossible to move anywhere. Eventually, I made love to Suzy and just after midnight Francis and I left with the promise to meet after daybreak. When we arrived home, we found Francis had a message from his Romanian girl friend that she wanted to visit him. Because Ramona's two children from her previous relationship to a white man had returned from their grandma's, and Suzy and I could no longer use their room, Francis decided to let me take Suzy to his friend Hussein's place.

The friendship between Francis and Hussein was so tight they had keys to each other's homes. Hussein, who with his dreadlocks and love for reggae music looked more like a Jamaican than a Sudanese, had gone to Frankfurt to spend some time with his Ethiopian girlfriend. About midday, Francis drove me to Ramona's place where we picked up Suzy. After we stopped at McDonalds to purchase some Chicken McNuggets, Francis dropped us at Hussein's place and immediately Suzy and I went to work. We had so much fun we just couldn't stop. The chemistry between us was so good; it was as if we had known each other for years. But everything has an end, and we were no exception, so we finally got exhausted and gave in.

The plan was for Suzy to return to her town and the two of us would meet on the weekend. Francis arrived just behind schedule to pick us up and we dropped Suzy at the train station.

Two days later I had just returned to my refugee home

from work and was preparing to leave for Francis' place, when the phone rang. One of the few Albanians I was still on good terms with picked up the phone and said it was my call.

"Ali." The voice sounded strange but I recognized it as Francis.

"Ali, I just can't believe it. This couldn't be happening."

Round and round he went, not making much sense. I gathered something was wrong, but not what. "Suzy's dead. Ramona just told me."

"What? You're joking?"

"No, it's true."

"What? What happened?"

"I don't know. She was crying so much when she told me…Ramona, I mean. You'll have to ask her."

I called Ramona, but she was so hysterical and emotional, I couldn't understand what she was saying.

"Ramona, Ramona," I said. "Look, I'll call you later, okay?" And I hung up.

I called her later in the night from Francis' place.

"Suzy died from a drug overdose," Ramona said. She sounded all cried out, at least for now.

"How did it happen?" I asked.

"A boyfriend gave her some drugs and maybe they were bad. Anyway, she OD'd."

I knew that Suzy was dead. I had further confirmation the following day from a local newspaper, which gave a full account of events leading to her sudden death.

Unfortunately, I didn't learn until after her death that she and Ramona became friends while both were undergoing rehabilitation for drug addiction. The week I met her was her last before starting her probation. Birds of a feather, they say fly together. This was obvious in this case. But as I mourned her, I cursed myself for not being more reasonable and finding additional information about her before heading into that short-lived relationship. In any case, I felt for Suzy, and the day of her death will forever remain one of the saddest in my life.

EIGHT

11th Hour Escape from Deportation

It seemed to me that Stefan was so paranoid he wouldn't listen to reason. He appeared determined to get me out of Germany – despite the attempts of my employers and the senior officer to keep me there. Stefan scheduled my return home for February 25, 1999. On the eve of my scheduled departure, I visited my lawyer, and according to him, the appeals court judge ruled in my refugee claim that I had exhausted any right to request political asylum in Germany until three years after the rejection of my first claim. According to him that day fell on February 26, 1999, a day after my scheduled departure. My lawyer believed my request would be granted for many reasons

As the judge's ruling suggests, three years is the maximum probation for a claimant to wait before making another claim. That is if the claimant still remains in the country. It is fair to say that the three-year period is set deliberately, because usually a rejected individual is sent home long before. So, this time span is made with the belief the claimant would be long gone at the three-year end. That was one plus for me. Secondly, the Bundesamt had acknowledged my identity, which was crucial. Another big plus was my living in Germany for three years without a criminal record.

However, the problem was getting through the next twenty-four hours, because I would become an illegal alien if I failed to report February 25 at the airport and could be subject to forced deportation. But if I left, I'd lose out on any political asylum for three years. It was Catch-22.

I decided to follow in my friends' footsteps – move to a neighbouring country. I arranged with a friend, living in the State of North Rhine Westphalia, to take me across the border to the Netherlands to stay with another friend. So on the day of my scheduled departure from Germany, I bought a train ticket and headed north of the Rhine River.

Back at my refugee home, the Kosovo Albanians were happy and celebrating my departure. They thought I had been deported. When a friend from the United States whom I routinely kept in touch with, called, they told her I had been deported back to Africa.

As I arrived at the first lap of my journey, at my friend's place in the Ruhr Rhine area, "the industrial heartland of Germany," this friend changed his mind. He thought it would be in my best interest to stay with him instead of proceeding to the Netherlands. At first I was scared because I thought the authorities would be looking for me, which they usually do when a refugee claimant avoids deportation and escape. But after my friend had convinced me that others had survived this situation the same way, I decided to stay.

Anyway, I had to wait for my belongings to arrive. I couldn't risk carrying them with me on the train in case the police checked my ID. So, before leaving, I had moved my possessions to Francis' place. He had agreed to forward them to me and I had paid him for this. But weeks after my arrival, he hadn't made any attempt to do so. I wondered if he had a hidden agenda and was taking advantage of my situation. I later learned this was the case.

To the rescue came my German connection, Julia, and her mother who lived in the same town as Francis. Mother and daughter took charge of my belongings and made sure I had them a few weeks later. Here is a situation that goes against the usual belief of white bashers that white people are racist, wicked, intolerable and stingy. I had given my so-called friend, Francis, a black man, money to transport my luggage and he kept the money and the luggage until I asked a white friend, Julia, to step in. In fact when I called her and told her my situation, she was angry that I had not brought my stuff to her house in the first place. Clearly, she was showing appreciation for the help I had given them to renovate the building her late dad had left them.

Meanwhile it was déjà vu all over again. Just like in Saudi Arabia, I had once again become an illegal alien. Before I could settle down, I started looking for ways to survive. Four weeks into my stay, my host said he had obtained a job for me at a McDonald's which was located in *Haupt Bahnhoff,* the city's main train station.

"You mean McDonald's, the world renowned fast food restaurant?" I asked.

"Yes, McDonald's," he said. "Come. I'll drive you there." He steered me towards his car.

As we made our way, I began to feel uneasy. My discomfort escalated when we arrived at Haupt Bahnhoff. The entire place was filled with people arriving and departing, purchasing tickets, meeting loved ones. And the police were everywhere. My mind darted all over the place. How could I make it every day going past the German police when I knew they were notorious for making on-the-spot ID checks, especially if you were black? That was my first sign of trouble.

As my host sat me down and went to get some McDonald's burgers, I speculated on the nature of my job and how the hell I would do it when I did not have legal documents. After we finished our burgers, he took me towards the restaurant's washrooms where a fellow black man appeared to be working. A few minutes after introduction, my host said, "this is where you are going to work."

A janitorial job. Not bad, I thought. However, I wasn't on anyone's payroll. The system was different from what I had seen anywhere. McDonald's in the city wasn't directly hiring janitors to clean their washrooms. My host explained that janitorial work used to be done by their regular staff, who combined it with their regular services. However, due to customer complaints on hygiene grounds, the fast food chain was forced to change the practice of letting their staff clean the toilets simultaneously with performing their restaurant services.

Somehow, a few Africans had convinced the McDonald's managers that they could get people to do the janitorial work free of charge. The plan the Africans presented to McDonald's did allow the janitors to make a living – from the customers. This plan called for a notice to be placed on the washroom doors. This notice told customers to donate to the janitors any amount they felt was fair if they were happy with the washrooms' conditions.

It was bizarre, but I did it for 12 hours a day. The washrooms had to be cleaned at least every five to 10 minutes amid the worse case scenario of not knowing whether I would make some money or not. For me, personally, it was a difficult situation because unlike my friends who were bold and often solicited the users personally for money, I am a very shy guy. To stand there and ask for money made me feel very uncomfortable.

It was really panhandling; the only difference was we worked hard. Some days were good, especially when there had been city events such as soccer matches. Other days were just heartbreaking, especially when some customers thought it was wrong to pay to use the washrooms. Some of these people often tried to make trouble. Guess who these troublemakers were? They were mostly non-African Blacks, East Indians, Chinese, Latinos, and other visible minorities. On the other hand, the Germans usually had a lot of sympathy for us and donated generously on certain occasions such as during soccer matches.

This situation took on other peculiarities. The washrooms were junkie and prostitute central so that brought in the police and secret police. The place definitely was unsuitable for an illegal alien to be. However, the police believed we were working legally, so they asked for our assistance. They urged us to prevent prostitutes and drug users/dealers from staying in the washrooms longer than necessary. But as illegal aliens we lived in a precarious situation especially when the police needed us as witnesses because drug users either overdosed or bloodied the floor with their needles, or in the worse case, someone died while sitting on the toilet.

In spite of all the fear and anxiety, I managed to survive, thanks mostly to the liberal policies of the administrators in North Rhine Westphalia. Unlike Bavaria, this state under the Rhine Valley was like any other modern dynamic place. Not only was it the most industrialized and most populous state, with the largest and finest cities such as Düsseldorf, Cologne, Dortmund, and Bonn in the German federation, it was also a state that prided itself as a model of diversity, tolerance and multiculturalism. Only a few countries around the globe could compare to its metropolitan nature.

So, I hoped that one day I would secure a more respectable job. In the summer of 1999, I had a hint from my host's younger brother. Little brother was also looking for work and regularly visited the *Arbeitsamt,* (Government Employment office). This time he learned that a four-star hotel was hiring dishwashers. I went there to try my luck and met with the chef.

"I understand you're hiring dishwashers and I'd like to apply for that position," I said.

"Yes, that's true. We do need dishwashers. But I'd like to hire you to be a breakfast cook. You can be part of my breakfast team, preparing breakfast for our guests."

"You're kidding me?" My mouth hung open. I'd never had the slightest idea about being a cook and I wasn't sure how welcoming that would be for a black man working as a cook in a first class hotel.

"Uh, I've never been a cook and have no prior experience as one." "Doesn't matter. We'll train you. You'll just have to be smart and learn fast. But you strike me as someone who would have no problem with this."

So there I was the following day fully equipped in my cooker's gear. I was introduced to a middle-aged German lady, Petra, who was in charge of the breakfast detail. She was my co-worker and trainer. Thankfully, the situation wasn't as difficult as I had anticipated. Within a week I had learned more than the rudiments and greatly exceeded expectation. The lady was impressed with me and happy to have me working there because I had eased her from some responsibilities. For example, before I was employed, she usually had to report to work very early in the morning to open the kitchen and make preparations. Fortunately for her, that became my responsibility.

However, as I started to gain a foothold in the hotel, jealousy and racism began to set in big time. Along with this German lady and I, there were students doing their on-the-job training to become cooks. They were not fulltime workers.

They worked on specific days and spent other days in school over time, these students became hostile. Soon it was clear that they begrudged going to school to become cooks while I appeared to have the job handed to me on a silver platter. It didn't help that I was black and they were Turks, Bosnians, and Russian Germans. While I made significant progress and received much praise from the chef and Petra, the detractors plotted against me.

And to paraphrase, like a stew, the plot thickened. Jorgen, the assistant chef, who was on vacation when I started work, returned. I soon discovered that Jorgen was another Stefan. Jorgen began creating many problems for me. First, he didn't like the idea that I was employed as a cook when I didn't have the proper cooking education. He also resented that the chef constantly praised me. But the bottom line was he didn't like the idea of a black man being a cook in his kitchen. He was also a very good friend of this middle-aged woman who had come to like me so much. He seemed to have so much influence on her that she followed everything he told her, despite her being much older than him.

There was also intense rivalry between him and Petra on one hand, and the chef on the other hand. I was later told by two German girls working in the hotel's front office – Jeannette and Silke – whose close relationship with me was another reason for Jorgen's behaviour – that the enmity was political. The chef came from the eastern part of Germany and Jorgen and Petra resented being under the control of an easterner.

Most Westerners regarded Easterners as inferior mainly because of the economic disparity between the East and West Germans. And the friendship between Jorgen and Petra had started long before the arrival of the chef who hired me. The former two had hoped that Jorgen would be promoted to chef. Anyway, Jorgen continued to cause me all sorts of problems, including blatant acts of sabotage. Some of these acts could have cost the hotel dearly, had I not been resilient and shown some resolve.

In this part of Germany, soccer was very popular and had scores of impassioned followers. Because the hotel was first class, it attracted world-class guests, including many of these soccer teams. On one of the hotel's busiest days, when the hotel was full with a visiting soccer team, fans and celebrities, Jorgen took his outrageous acts to a new level. The day before we were given the list of hotel guests to be served for breakfast. Naturally, moral was high and everyone geared up in full anticipation of the day.

The day arrived. Early that morning I made my regular early entry to open the kitchen. As usual I went to the reception, signed in and collected the keys. But along with the keys was a note from Silke which stated that Petra had called in sick and advised me to get personnel from room service to assist me.

Huh? I scratched my head.

I had no doubts that Jorgen had engineered this scenario and so did Petra. (I still have the note of the message Silke had given me.) It wasn't the first time he'd pulled off this stunt. Previously, when Petra had taken a short vacation and I was paired with some of the students, Jorgen had urged them to stay away. Remember, these students were jealous of me because of my status, so they listened to Jorgen.

But this time was different because of the full hotel. This time showed how low Jorgen could go, that he could succeed in convincing Petra to do his bidding, when the hotel was full.

No way was I going to let Jorgen's evil intentions disgrace me. If he had hoped to dampen my spirits and moral and force me to give in, I was going to squash those hopes. As soon as I changed into my cooking gear, I went to business. I looked at my watch – 5 a.m. I had only two hours to prepare breakfast and deliver it into the restaurant.

I went straight to the food preparation area and switched on all the ovens and the cookers. I placed two huge frying pans on two of the cookers and poured cooking oil in both of them. I hurried to one of the cold rooms, grabbed some fresh eggs, cracked them in a bowl, stirred them and poured them into the pans. Then, I transferred fresh bacon into the ovens.

Once I had all the meals that required heating, frying, and cooking ready, I moved to dairy and other liquid. Sandy, a Filipino friend who worked at the Banquet and Winter Garden, helped me transfer the liquid products –milk, coffee, juice – to the hotel restaurant. I also began moving the different kind of breads, baguette, sliced and the cereals, cookies and fruits, respectively. At all times, I kept a close eye on the bacon and the scrambled eggs.

At this point, I had completed about eighty percent of the job. Now I could start arranging the fruit salad, sliced roasted beef, salmon, salami, cheese etc. on a 12"x 18" stainless plate. A small space is left at the top of the plate for salad leaves. On top of the salad leaves, the back of peeled tomatoes and oranges are set up to resemble roses.

For the fruit decoration I used skills that Jorgen and Petra had taught me. I cut a watermelon into two, making the edges of the two parts resemble the teeth of a band saw blade. Then I scooped out the melon, leaving a hole, which I filled with a mixture of sliced pineapple, apples, oranges, tangerines, strawberries and grapes. Then it was back to the bacon and scrambled eggs, now cooked. I carried them to the restaurant and began to prepare the back-up meals. This was essential because sometimes the hotel guests streamed in continuously and we couldn't afford to let them hang around without anything to eat. With perseverance and determination, I did the unexpected almost single-handedly and on time.

Everything was so orderly, when the chef arrived about 90 minutes later; it took him almost two hours to realize that Petra hadn't come in. He found out only after he had attended the routine meeting of the hotel. I was so happy with my achievement and performance that I didn't bother to tell him what had transpired. I wanted him to figure it out himself.

Not surprisingly, he was furious when he found out. He was also pleased that I had saved the day and that no disruption or delay had occurred. He was so proud he decided to let me leave two hours early as the students and other afternoon staff had arrived by midday. But I stayed on and worked my full shift. I had to show him the respect he deserved and my defiance to Jorgen. Jorgen would have to find this out second hand. Like his co-conspirator, he had played hooky.

As the days passed, I hoped that Jorgen would change. I tried to reconcile with him. On half a dozen occasions, the chef called Jorgen and me into his office, sometimes in the senior staff meeting room.

"Why aren't you two getting along?" The chef looked first at Jorgen, then at me.

"What?" asked Jorgen? "You must be mistaken. I like Ali. He is very hard working."

"Well, then, shake hands," the chef said. And we did.

One surprising circumstance about Jorgen – he usually treated me decently and with respect whenever the chef was on vacation or sick leave. It made me wonder whether it was his hatred for the chef that spilt over to include me. But the backfiring of his plots seemed to enrage him more. It reached the point where he drew a wedge between Petra and me. Petra was married to a Senegalese man and because he is black, I thought it was common sense for her to try to convince Jorgen to like me. However, because of Jorgen's influence on her, she was unable to tell him to back off from his racist behaviour.

"He's a racist," I said to Petra.

"No. Don't ever call him that. If it weren't for him I wouldn't have this job." Her face was turning red. She shook the stirring spoon at me and scowled. Her face matched the tomato sauce she had been making.

"It's true," I said. "You remember, Mardi, the Gambian guy that worked here. Jorgen treated him the same way."

"Well, what did you expect? Mardi was always yelling at him and calling him a racist."

"Because he is."

"No, he isn't and I don't want to hear anymore about it." She turned away, stuck the spoon into the pot and began whipping the sauce.

Because of my status, there was nothing I could do but accommodate his stupid behaviour, even when he escalated it. Every time I went to the locker room to change and I met him, he said something bad about me. One day we got into a shouting match.

"Neo-Nazi," I called him.

He turned around from the cutting board. His mouth hung open and he dropped the knife from his hand. He stood still for a few seconds, then his face did a slow burn and his mouth closed into a snarl.

"I'll sue you," he said. He bent down, retrieved the knife and began chopping onions staccato style.

The writing was on the wall for me as far as my employment there, but not before I suffered one more memorable embarrassment and humiliation. This time the perpetrator was a hotel guest of Far East Asian origin. He refused to accept the meal he had ordered because I, a black man was serving him.

Despite all these problems at work, I continued to have fun with my lovely German girls. I was able to kiss and hug my girlfriends where I wanted, when I wanted – in the streets, on the hood of their cars, at the clubs, or at the restaurants, anywhere. Even at my place of work. We were doing it without anybody making it his or her business.

Unlike my previous residence, no one driving by in a car threatened me. And relations with the police were amicable with only one slight bump. One day they stopped me to check for my ID. I told them I had forgotten it at home, and after a few questions, they accepted my answer. This was in sharp contrast to what was going on in Bavaria where an ID check, particularly of black people, was a daily routine.

However, after almost three years playing hide and seek, I decided to move to Canada, the country where I had always wanted to live.

NINE

Canada - My Dream Country

Canada has fascinated me since I was in my early teens and I always hoped that some day I could make it my home. My enthrallment with the country has its roots in my elementary school geography class.

It wasn't the maps; the Canadian way of life or the diversified climate that first captured my interest, but the teacher's unique pronunciations of Canadian provinces and landmarks. To him, Newfoundland was pronounced "Nu Fuuland." Also names such as Saskatchewan, (Saskatchswine) and Saskatoon (Saskatuu-une). Thanks to this teacher, Canada became a household name in class. I was hooked. I had no choice. I had to come to Canada.

That dream came true in late December 2001. Then I arrived at Toronto's Pearson Airport and sought political asylum. I was met at the airport by Mariam, whom I had known for many years back in Ghana. I lived with her for the first three months of my arrival before I moved to my current place of residence.

But I soon found that landing in a beautiful country didn't guarantee a smooth ride. I began to have a feeling of déjà vu as some of the Germany experiences repeated themselves. Perhaps, I could rationalize that because Germany was involved, that was why these events occurred. Perhaps for the first incident that was true. But certainly not the rest.

Again, I was forced to leave my personal belongings in Germany. I had to enter Canada the same way I entered Germany – using another person's document, this time a German passport. I felt a sense of urgency to get my personal ID and other documents to back up my refugee claims and to avoid the fate I suffered in Germany.

But here in Canada, I had more than two non-working days to get my documents and to prepare for my hearing. I had been in Canada for a couple of months before Canadian Immigration officials invited me for my first interview. This interview would determine my eligibility to make a refugee claim and to have it referred to the Immigration and Refugee Board, the Canadian body that oversees all refugee claims inside Canada.

But due to my long circuitous trip from Germany, through Belgium, the Netherlands, and finally to Canada, my resources were very limited.

So, I sent some money via Western Union, (supposedly the safest and most tactical way) to my friend in Germany to ship my belongings to me. But like a hound from hell, an unfortunate sequence of events also pursued me in Canada. Several calls over several days to my friend in Germany revealed only non-receipt of my money. I decided to call the toll-free inquiry number on the Western Union receipt. The Western Union rep began bombarding me with questions. I figured he needed the information to trace my money. Wrong.

"Sorry, the money can't be released because you're on the United States government terrorist watch list," he said.

"What? There must be some mistake."

"Nope. But if you fax me your ID showing your place of birth and country of origin, then we can release your money."

This didn't sound like a Western Union representative.

"Where are you?" I asked.

"Kentucky."

"What? I thought I was speaking to a Western Union rep in Canada."

"No, sir. Kentucky. Now, I repeat, we've red-flagged your order until you send in your ID."

"What are you? CIA or FBI?" I raised my voice. "You're only doing this because I'm Muslim."

"No, sir. I'm not."

"Yes, you are. Come on. The transaction is only for $300U.S. It doesn't make sense. You're discriminating against me because I'm Muslim. What's the matter with you? You can't…"

"Sir, calm down. I am not discriminating against you."

"Yes, you are. I demand that you release my money now."

"Sir, I can't do that until you send me your ID."

"That's discrimination. I'm going to the human rights board over this. You can't do this."

"Sir, sir, calm down."

"Calm down. I'll calm down when you release my transaction money." I slammed down the phone.

The following day I reported him to the Canadian Human Rights Commission. They advised me I had no choice but to do as requested – fax copies of my ID to the office concerned. What a let down. Worse, I later found the fax destination was not Western Union but the United States Homeland and Security Department. I also tried to report this incident to the Toronto Police Services but the officer who took my call gave me the same advice. He cited the post 9/11 world that we live in. However, he said they could step in if I sent the fax and the money was not released or refunded. I had no choice. I trudged over to the branch office of Western Union, and gave them my ID to be faxed to the Homeland and Security Department.

Besides seeing this as racial profiling, I was also concerned about sending my ID to someone I didn't know at an unknown office. Identity theft was on the rise and it could be anyone at the end of the fax. However, after a few minutes, the person on the other end confirmed receipt; I was cleared and the red flag was removed, so I could call my friend in Germany to pick up the money.

But I wouldn't leave quietly. I felt embarrassed and humiliated. No way was I going to let this fellow get away with his treatment of me or let it happen again. Besides I had a lot of personal stuff, including my stereo and CDs, coming from Germany. So, I lit into the man at the end of the phone.

"Fascist. Neo-Nazi," I shouted into the receiver. I didn't care that the Western Union rep behind the counter was probably staring at me. "Persecutor of Muslims."

"Hey, hey, sir," the Homeland and Security Department fellow said. I could hear his intake of breath through the line. "Look, I'll give you a reference number which you can quote any time you send money via Western Union."

If I thought that was the end of this fiasco, I was living in Never-never land. My friend in Germany collected the money all right, but then he didn't send me my belongings. Again, I had to fork out more money and waste more time to retrieve most of my belongings. Once more I was forced to solicit the services of an ex-girlfriend to get my possessions shipped to me.

Meanwhile, thanks to Canada's generous refugee system, the Canadian authorities didn't give me a deadline to get my documents. However, as expected, after a couple of months, they gave me notice to appear before a senior Immigration Officer for an interview to decide my eligibility for refugee status. It turned out to be positive. My claim was then referred to the Immigration and Refugee Board. Perhaps things were taking a turn for the better. After I had fulfilled all the required formalities of taking and passing a medical examination, receiving a work permit and then a social insurance number, I began looking for a job.

The search wasn't as easy as I thought it would be. As I struggled to find work, I had an uncomfortable feeling that it was my Muslim name which turned off prospective employers. More disappointing and depression were the sources of this discrimination and profiling. Not only white people were doing it, but also visible minorities, the same people who would normally complain about being victims of racial discrimination.

My first job was at a very small company, which dealt in second-hand clothing. The company had a huge warehouse where second hand clothing, mostly bought from the United States, was baled in bundles and shipped to Africa to be sold. My job was to operate one of the machines used to bale the clothing. I was there for obvious reasons, to give me time to put things in order as I searched for a much more established company where I hoped to work for a long time. This job also provided me with some money so I could eat and pay rent.

My Canadian host, Mariam, tipped me off that the sister company where she worked had an opening and was hiring skilled labour, mainly welders. I thought it was a good opportunity for me. In Ghana, after my four years technical and polytechnic education I had received my intermediate certificate in welding and metallurgy in 1982, and the advanced level one in 1985; both were issued by the City and Guilds of London Institute. When I arrived in Canada I enrolled at a technical institute in east Toronto where I obtained a certificate and the Ontario provincial license after a three-week course.

Early the next morning, I showed up at this company because I didn't want to blow the opportunity. As I sat on a bench outside their premises, waiting for the offices to be opened, a guy who claimed to be a company employee joined me.

We sat in silence for a few minutes and then we started talking.

"Are you here for one of the welders' jobs?" he asked.

"Yes," I replied. "I have the provincial welder's license, so I figured I'd have a good chance of getting hired." I smiled. "Do you know how many openings there are?

"Well, one for sure. You could even be in for some luck because I have to leave. My father just died, so I have to go back home to Guyana to sort things out."

"Oh, I'm sorry."

"Hmm. Well, you should also not have a problem because the Human Resources Manager is a Jamaican black lady from the Caribbean. She's an Evangelical Christian and a very good woman."

"Hmm."

I was a bit concerned. True, I'd maintained good relationships with Evangelical Christians in my homeland and elsewhere, but since 9/11, most Evangelicals were extremely hostile to Muslims. Unfortunately, this included discrimination of Muslims by many African Americans and Caribbean Africans.

So, there I sat, with mixed feelings of hope and dread. Then the doors opened and I walked into the building. I approached the receptionist, an elderly white lady, in the front office.

"Yes. May I help you?" She smiled at me.

"Yes. I'm Mohammed Ali and I'd like to apply for one of the welders' positions."

"Oh. Are you a Muslim?"

"Yes."

"Oh, I see." Her smile changed to a frown and she busied herself flipping through the papers on her desk.

"I'd like to fill out an application form," I said.

She fidgeted with the papers some more, then pulled one out and shoved it at me.

"Here. Make sure you fill out every line." She returned to the papers on her desk.

I walked back to my chair and started doing just that. Occasionally I looked up and noticed the company staff filtering into the front office. To my horror, I discovered they seemed to follow the same procedure. One of them would pop into the waiting room; stare at me as if I had Mr. Spock ears, then return to his or her office.

I thought I heard voices murmuring down the hall. I looked up and noticed that the receptionist wasn't at her desk. I caught on. It was now very clear that the receptionist had told them something about me and that something was my name and my religion.

I couldn't wait until the Human Resources Manager met me.

I continued filling out the application and handed it and my other documents to the receptionist who had now returned to her desk. She began flipping through my papers and stopped to read a reference letter from the German senior citizens home. As I didn't want to appear nosey, I started walking back to my chair. Just then, a middle-aged black lady entered the reception. She looked at me with a gentle smile. I smiled back and sat down. She turned to the hall, presumably to go to her office. The receptionist jumped from her chair, grabbed my papers, and hurried after the black lady.

I could feel a shift in attitude. It had to be that letter of reference. The language in it was so powerful and it must have moved the elderly receptionist. Now she wanted me to be employed.

Meanwhile, as I still sat waiting, the Human Resources Manager came out, leaned over the receptionist's desk and whispered something to her. Then she turned around, squinted at me, nodded her head a couple of time, then returned to her office.

"Come here," the receptionist said to me.

I stood up and went over to her desk.

"The Human Resources Manager will contact you in a few days." Her voice seemed to hold a promise.

However, I never heard back from either of them. No doubt, it was the prerogative of the human resources to hire me or refuse me, regardless of whether they needed workers urgently or not. But it was clear to me that I got rejected because of my religion. It came as no surprise because I had similar encounters prior to this particular company. Things became so bad, some of my friends suggested that I change my name if I wanted to live happily in North America and work in an established company.

As my search to work in a more established company continued, I sent my résumé to an employment agency in Brampton, Ontario. When I made a follow-up call a few days later, a man who claimed to be a Canadian of Greek origin picked up the phone.

"My agency cannot help you because of a "Christian thing," he said.

"What do you mean by that?"

"Well, er, just company policy. However, there may be a

way around this. I can give you the name of a company where I worked before. It's owned by a Muslim and I believe that the majority of the workers are Muslims."

"That would be good." I said. "I can pass along a good word about you."

"No, no, no," he said. I could hear him spit out the words. "You cannot tell anybody where you got this information. You must give me your word that you won't let anybody know I've sent you to the company."

Maybe he was concerned he would be fired if his bosses discovered he had directed me to a company without going through the agency. After all, his salary came from the commission employers seeking staff paid the agency.

"I won't tell," I said. "I give you my word."

"Okay. Here's the contact information and I'll give you directions to the company." And he did. "I have to warn you the working conditions aren't that good. The place is very dusty, so you won't want to stay there too long. But it's a good deal for you. The pay is $14 an hour, which you won't get from most agencies."

"Thank you," I replied.

I faxed my résumé to the company where he had referred me. Within a few hours, the owner of the company called me for an assessment and interview. True to the Greek fellow's predictions I was offered employment. However, as soon as I was hired, I found out that the boss was not a Muslim; neither did a Muslim own the company, and there were no Muslims working there. In fact, for years I remained the only Muslim in the company.

However, I did figure out why the Greek fellow had concluded the company was owned by a Muslim and had many Muslim employees. The boss was an East Indian and the majority of the workers were Sikhs. Because their turbans and other dress code looked similar to some Muslims in the Middle East and Southeast Asian regions, it was easy to understand his mistake.

As unfortunate as it might seem, this is what our world had come to. The Greek fellow's error served as a reminder of the ignorance and prejudice many people still harbour, said ignorance and prejudice, I believe, most often the root cause of bigotry, hatred and, of course, racial discrimination.

A case in point is an incident which occurred in Mesa, a suburb of Phoenix, Arizona, on September 15, 2001. In this aftermath of 9/11, a Sikh man was gunned down in a rage because the attacker had mistaken him for a Muslim. Even if he were a Muslim, does that make what happened right?

Fast forward to four years later and another encounter with Western Union. This time I had wired 55 Euros to Germany for a friend to forward my remaining CDs and speakers. As previously transpired, the money was put on hold. This time, though, despite Homeland Security's authorization to release the money, Western Union in Germany refused to comply, even after my friend presented my ID, which I had sent her. I had no choice but to take my money back.

With this worldwide demand for personal information, the real danger Muslims like me face is where is our personal information going to land? Will it end up in the wrong hands and be used for malicious purposes? I only pray for the love of God to save us from this madness; otherwise innocent lives will continue to suffer as victims of injustices – all because of their names and the color of their skin.

TEN

Monkey Slur

The East Indians' weren't the only employees of this company. Others, mainly of Indian origin, came from the West Indies. The combination of these two groups worried me. From my experience traveling and living in other countries, I found that these two groups of people can be some of the most viciously racist. As I mentioned in earlier chapters, I have suffered racism, verbal and otherwise, but not the kind or on the scale I suffered from these two groups. So, with the two groups together in one place, I expected double trouble. Not the physical kind, but words, which can hurt. To paraphrase the words of Robert Fulghum, author of All I Need to Know I Learned in Kindergarten[1] – *Sticks and stones may break my bones, but words may break my heart.*

The worst of these words came from the mouth of Ravig, a Guyanese fellow of Indian origin. My African supervisor, who was married to a black Guyanese, had warned me how racist people with this mixed background can be. However, I never thought Ravig would be so stupid and insensitive as he was one afternoon.

On this bright summer afternoon, I opted to eat my lunch

in an isolated area within the company's premises. All of a sudden I saw Ravig coming towards me. He was bald with a dark complexion – in some quarters he would be referred to as black. He sat beside me and asked me questions about Africa.

"I'd like to visit Africa one day," he said.

Right, I thought. I knew where he was going and it wasn't a love of Africa. I could feel my sandwich jumping around in my stomach and the sweat forming on my forehead.

"The only problem I think I'll have in Africa is understanding the language of your brothers," he said.

"What do you mean by that?" I swallowed hard. "Africans have hundreds of languages."

"Hee-hee. Wuu, wuu, wuu." He then moved his hands to imitate how monkeys climb trees.

I looked him up, and down, with such anger; it was as if somebody had threatened to take my soul away. I continued staring at him while weighing my options on an appropriate response. Physically, he was no match and I could beat him to death with very little effort. But I am not a violent person. I also was a refugee and I felt any altercation could damage my records and might be used against me at my hearing. It could also cause the refusal of my refugee claim and subsequent deportation.

At the same time, I thought I needed to punish him somehow, so he would learn a lesson and never again say to another human being what he had said to me. My other option was to report him to the company authorities, but I figured he would deny making such comments because there was no witness. So I strongly leaned towards beating the hell out of him to teach him a lesson and to console my wounded soul.

But thank God I did not, and I thank Him for giving me the patience he gave me that day. Otherwise, I could be languishing in jail today. The bottom line, though, is thank

God I was able to keep my cool and not overreact and do something stupid. But I still feel very hurt and wonder how the man had the audacity to refer to me as a monkey.

Unfortunately, the racist program against me continued every day. It escalated every time one of the men saw me talk to a female from their community. Our conversation might have nothing to do with love and romance; most of the time it was work-related questions – perhaps some directions or technical help required. But you'd think I was planning rape because as soon as the woman and I finished our conversation, one of her male colleagues would corner her and give her the third degree. I know this from eavesdropping or hearing about it from the women.

Last July, I made the mistake of offering two East Indian young women, a ride home after work because they lived near me. They'd no sooner entered my car, when an old Indian man sitting in his SUV, climbed out and approached the young and tried to persuade them to get out. The young ladies snubbed the old man, so I took off and drove them to their home.

The following day, as I climbed in my car after work, I saw the two ladies standing at a bus stop across the street. I slowed down to give them a ride, but they waived me to drive on. I thought they had alternative means of transportation, so continued my journey. The third day, though, as I was heading home, I saw them standing at an intersection about 150 yards from our company. This time, they stopped me and asked for a ride. During the journey home they told me the trash talk they've been getting and how their fellow women poked fun at them for riding in a black monkey's car, etc.

Meanwhile, according to the young ladies, the old man and his fellow Indians refused to drive them near their home on grounds that they lived in Brampton or downtown Mississauga.

There were also numerous instances where racial slurs were used against me but they were phrased like a greeting or a very kind word. Only on further investigation afterwards, did I discover that the word or words meant "monkey" or some equally offensive word. It was déjà vu, like I was back in Saudi Arabia.

Sometimes it appeared to happen in waves. A few months after the first Guyanese had provoked me with those monkey remarks, another one made similar comments, this time, indirectly, but I had no doubt he was referring to me. The scenario went like this:

I was the company's tool room keeper, so it was my responsibility to issue tools to the staff. That morning, this Guyanese guy Mohanne wanted to borrow some tools. While I dealt with him, another fellow came in. This second guy was mentally unsound and a constant target of the others' mockery. So, when Mohanne started in, I thought that was it. But Mohanne's words were filled with profanity and were so offensive, I can't repeat them. The gist of it referred to the second fellow as being from the jungle and living in trees with monkeys and other animals. The words could have forced me to beat him up, but because he directed the remarks towards the other guy, and not me, I could not. But I stared him up and down as if I was going to hit him.

"Where does your er, friend, come from? I asked Mohanne. I figured they were both of West Indian origin.

"Oh, man, we're both from Guyana. Same city."

Now, I began to suspect I was the target of those remarks, because some of the West Indian guys at work had used them routinely when referring to Black Africans. "You better watch what you are saying." I pointed a finger at him. "You could get into trouble. I don't want to hear anymore of those disgusting words. If I do hear them again; if you say anything derogatory to me or to anyone else here, I will show you my true colors and how a real jungle life is. I'm giving you fair warning." I leaned forward as if I was going to grab him.

Mohanne jumped back, turned and darted from the room. After that, whenever he saw me coming he tried to steer clear of me; if he couldn't, he faked a smile at me and hurried on his way.

Usually, I avoid generalization in criticizing racial groups. It is my hope that no racial group would feel unfairly targeted. It is more important to tell people the truth and make them take responsibility for their actions. As I have said, many different racial groups have used racial slurs against other Black Africans and me, but none so vicious as that of the Indians from East Asia or the West Indies, Hispanics, Latinos, Chinese, Arabs, Africans north of the Sahara Desert or from the Horn of Africa. These ethnic groups seem to follow the philosophy of rating one race superior and another inferior. And skin color always plays a major part in their behaviour and conduct. From everything I have learned through my interactions with them, they concede to white superiority, but compete among themselves over who is superior. Whatever their differences, they all see blacks as the most inferior.

I have observed that South Asians, in particular, seem to have so much contempt for black people. I watched the way they behaved in Africa, Saudi Arabia, and Germany. For example, at the refugee center in Germany, we always lined up to collect our social assistance money, our clothing and food. Because the majority of the refugees were Africans and East Europeans, there were two queues: the Black Africans joined by the few Algerians, Moroccans and Iraqis in one, and the East Europeans in the other. The South Asians preferred to join the East Europeans and only when they were snubbed or shunned did they decide to join the Africans. This line change often drew taunts and laughter from the Africans.

Sadly, South Asians have the reputation of treating black people with indifference even when living in predominantly black countries. This behaviour could be rooted in India's lower and upper caste system. It's hard to tell. Unfortunately, this South Asian apathy has led to some grim consequences.

For instance, in Uganda, the then brutal dictator Idi Amin used the South Asians' indifference to deport them. The local Ugandans didn't like the dictator but were happy that he deported the South Asians, even though the latter had lived in the country all their lives and invested so much. The locals didn't just envy and resent the South Asians because of their good living and middle-class status; they also saw them as arrogant and racist.

Of course, that does not justify the actions of one of our generation's most brutal dictators. More proof shows in the consequences of their indifference and racist behaviour.

Similar situations have occurred in South Africa, too. Most blacks there are still bitter and are not happy with a lot of South Asians because of what was seen as their partial support for the then apartheid regime. Blacks, no matter what their political and tribal differences, such as the one existing between the African National Congress and the Pan African Congress, were unanimous in their opposition of the apartheid. This regime was based on racial superiority and denied native blacks their power to rule and determine their own destiny.

However, the South Asians, especially the so-called Indian Bourgeoisie (Indian Middle Class), were deeply involved in bribing and soliciting the white regime, which enabled them to either get their way or force the white regime to pass laws which tended to favour them over the native and majority blacks. This situation helped prolong the apartheid rule.

A typical example is the 1983 Constitutional Reform Law. This law allowed the colored and South Asian minority to participate on a limited basis in government, but in a separate and subordinate house of parliament. The majority black population were allowed only to become citizens of the purported independent homelands.

It is fair to say that some South Asians did participate in the struggle against apartheid rule, and this must be acknowledged, especially the anti-apartheid "Indian Congress." To be fair, they were themselves victims of racism especially when they were forced into townships due to the Group Area Act enacted by the apartheid regime. Yet, that negative perception of the South Asians continues to haunt Black Africans because of most of the former's bourgeoisie and racist life during the days of apartheid.

Furthermore, the former didn't do themselves any favours after the dissolution of the apartheid rule. During the country's first multi-party democratic elections, they voted overwhelmingly for the former white-led parties, namely, the Democratic Alliance and New National Party, whose officials were mainly from the former apartheid regime. This further antagonized the black populations who for years were suspicious of the intentions of the South East Asians.

The latter's supremacist behaviour also often raised tensions in countries such as Fiji where the indigenous population have often felt discriminated against by Indian settlers. However, as in the example I gave about these South Asians' conduct at the refugee centre in Germany, they did make a reversal during the 2004 elections by voting massively for the black-dominated Africa National Congress, if only because they realized that the black majority was irreversible..

I frequently speculate why they continue to make these errors of judgment, but at the same time, I believe that they see themselves as superior to blacks and prefer to align themselves with whites first and only make a U-turn when backed against the wall. Thank God, they did finally realize it was in their best interest to side with the majority no matter their skin color. With the black majority feeling betrayed by the South Asians and the apartheid system gone for good that was the only reasonable course they could take to avoid more resentment from the black population, because the latter would hurt their interest.

Unfortunately, there are disturbing reports that Black South Africans are now engaged in racist acts against South Asians, especially the illegal immigrants who have been pouring into the country from India since apartheid's demise.

Another example of the importance of skin color to these ethnic groups is Chinese South Africans' resentment during the apartheid. They were not necessarily bitter from the apartheid itself. They were displeased because the apartheid regime classified people of Japanese and Taiwanese origin as honourable whites and permitted them the same privileges, but labeled mainland Chinese as Asians. From the Chinese point of view, that labeling made them appear the same as East Indians or South Asians, and they didn't like that. The mainland Chinese were so appalled being classified as South Asians, most of them left and settled in Vancouver, Canada.

Paradoxically, unlike the Germans or white people overall, there is no question the people of South Asia and the Far East are the most resentful of inter-racial marriage, especially when it involves a black person.

In previous chapters, I deliberately elaborated on my romance with the German girls, etc., not because I wanted to bluff or prove that I was a playboy or a womanizer, but to dispel the notion that racism is only a white man's thing. The fact of the matter is, despite all the myth about white-black tensions, inter-racial relationships between whites and blacks are some of the most common form of relationships in our world today, while black-Indian or black-Chinese relationships are almost non-existent. Some of these racial groups even consider it taboo for a member of their community to have any kind of romantic relationship with a black person.

All the above is against the backdrop of unqualified co-operation among governments of these racial groups'. For decades these governments have united against the perceived white domination and racism. At the United Nations, Non-Aligned Movement (NAM), etc, they have routinely taken a common stand.

Unfortunately, that government-to-government support and understanding, which help them achieve self-rule and independence from colonialism, imperialism and other issues of interest to them, has never been translated into mutual respect, person-to-person, in their racial differences.

The unfortunate scenario is that these are the groups – Chinese, Africans, Asians and Latinos, the alleged victims of white racism – who are supposed to be united against the perceived white racism. However, throughout my experiences, the first non-white people to complain about white racism are the South East Asians, Far East Asians and West Indians. When I am with them, I see it in their body language. They complain profusely when a white person is in our mixed group. They try to get some sympathy and solidarity. But as soon as their number doubles, they turn against me and begin their own name calling and racial slur.

Many people might ask, "What is so important with interracial marriages and racism?" While many believe that the institutionalized form of racism matters, such as Black Americans' fight for equal rights and opportunities, which, of course, must be sought, the worse form of racism is the person-to-person racial discrimination encountered by millions of people every second, every minute, every hour, every day.

There is nothing more upsetting than having to face racial discrimination or racial insults, daily, at your place of work, in a bus, at a public place, and in an elevator. Some of these routine forms of racism are so hurtful that at times I wonder and ask why God didn't create all mankind the same color – either all black or all white – so that we would not even have the word "racism," let alone having it become a menace to society. But as a man of faith, I believe in the judgment of the Almighty and I curse myself for even having that thought. But it is cruel, when a human being refers to another human being as a monkey.

The reason I applaud the interracial relationships and see them as a factor in the fight against racial discrimination is based on the axiom charity begins at home. In effect, it is through this person-to- person interaction that the backbone of racism can be broken. If a person can have an affair with another person of a different racial group without any qualms, it means there is acknowledgment of equality. Regardless of the superiority claimed by his or her race group, this person sees his or her partner not as a monkey or subhuman, but as a true member of the human race.

More worrisome is the attitude of non-white children towards a black person. From my experience, there is a huge difference between how I am received by white kids as compare to non-white, particularly, the Indian, Chinese and Hispanic kids. In Germany, I always had white children come to me asking for my autograph. It didn't matter where I was. I could be walking on the street, standing at a bus stop, etc. It's not because I was a super star or a celebrity.

To most of these kids, all blacks are the same – football stars, basketball star or rap stars. Therefore, once I came into their sight; they began calling me, invoking the names of some of the popular African soccer players in Europe. Others called me by the names of prominent African American super stars, such us Michael Jordan, Tupac Shakur, etc.

Even more touching was sometimes these kids became so impassioned and emotional; they forced their mothers to come begging to have my autograph. I have seen the same thing happen to my fellow blacks who were mere refugees.

Contrast that with the Hispanic, East Indian, West Indian and the Chinese kids that I meet, who tend to be rude and racist. Whether it is in an elevator, on the street or on public transport, their attitude and behaviour always appears as if they are in training to taunt a black person. Sometimes I even think this is the case. It is common to see a parent or a guardian, who is walking with a child, whisper in the child's ear. Then the child will either tease me by holding his or her nose to suggest I am something smelly, or engage in some other racist acts such as the monkey noises.

Sometimes I get so frustrated that I often ask myself why the system isn't like that of Bavaria, where everybody is a target. Because in Bavaria, as mentioned before, it doesn't matter whether you are black, white, Chinese or Mexican, as long as you are a foreigner, you face the same music. In that environment, there is no hypocrisy when complaining about racism. This situation is unlike that in Canada or elsewhere, where Latinos, South Asians, Chinese, Arabs, and Koreans can complain of racism while perpetuating it themselves, especially against black people.

But after those silly thoughts, I turn around and criticize myself for ever having considered a homogeneous system. There can never be any system equal to the Canadian one. It is a system which has vision. It is a system which treats humanity with dignity and respect, regardless of one's race, color or creed. That is what the Charter of Rights is all about. It is, therefore, a system that needs to be protected and preserved. However, the burden of making this system a springboard for other countries to emulate lies with the diverse ethnic groups.

Obviously, whoever believed that multiculturalism and diversity are bad needs some kind of therapy. Having said that, the indefatigable support of people from all the different ethnic backgrounds to help the government achieve its goals cannot be over-emphasized.

One thing that tends to undermine diversity and integration is the habit of different ethnic groups concentrate living in a particular area. This behaviour eventually makes these areas taboo for people of other races or ethnic groups. The result is that the whole idea of diversity, multiculturalism and tolerance seems like nonsense.

And that is what worries me about the future laws of countries such as Canada, which as mentioned, are doing everything to promote diversity and integration of various ethnic and racial groups. These ethnic groups are so entrenched in their cultural beliefs, it is very difficult to change them and have any meaningful integration.

Despite the government's genuine and ambitious undertakings, these new immigrants of various ethnic groups mostly seem to go their separate ways and prefer clinging to some of their archaic cultural values, instead of embracing modernization and Canadian values.

Of course, if you have an ethnic group which has a tradition of touchable and untouchables, it is hard for them to avoid discriminating against others who are not of their race, especially black people whom they consider inferior.

Equally significant is the attitude of these ethnic groups on the issue of dual citizenship. I sometimes wonder whether it is for the best. I do think it is a good thing and applaud countries such as Canada for implementing the system. However, sometimes the demeanour of these new citizens leaves a lot to be desired. It is often very hard to determine how loyal and patriotic they are to their new countries.

My personal opinion is that the loyalty of most of them often lies with their mother countries and this loyalty manifests during special occasions such as the world cup soccer. During these events in a city such as Toronto, it is always tough to tell which country you are living in. Instead of Canadian flags, you see the flags of the various countries representing the soccer teams, which are the countries where many of their fans originate. The scenes of jubilations sometimes are so absurd it can give people with xenophobic tendencies room to manoeuvre and to justify their hatred for non-native citizens and foreigners.

Of course, Canada is not one of the elite soccer nations. However, based on the behaviour of some of these soccer fans, I wonder where their loyalty would go if Canada qualified for a world cup final and had to play against countries that are the main sources of its immigration.

I don't want to be called paranoid, but I can safely say that, despite all the happiness and euphoria in obtaining Canadian citizenship, I think some people take citizenship of their new countries as a matter of convenience. If you look at the patriotism exhibited by citizens of other countries such as the United States, it becomes clear that most new citizens in Canada don't show that kind of enthusiasm and patriotism.

Of course, I am not advocating xenophobic or redneck-type patriotism, but I don't believe people should be taking Canadian citizenship for granted. The bottom line is that a lack of seriousness, a lack of pride and a lack of genuinely showing patriotism, only breeds' racist and anti-foreigner sentiments by right wing groups, and makes it problematic for prospective citizenship applicants. In a nutshell, I believe once immigrants and new Canadian citizens accept Canadian values, racial discrimination perpetuated by some ethnic groups will be history.

A startling discovery I have made about racism is that, while every racial group perpetuates it across the board, the ones most likely to engage in daily forms of racism tend to be overwhelmingly poor and uneducated non-whites. And that is where it stings the most. There is nothing more hurtful than seeing someone you regard as poor and illiterate, and empathize with, who has no self-respect. Instead of minding their own business and cleaning their stinky bodies and clothes, they try to look down upon other people because of their skin color.

While there is no question racial discrimination is common among the whites, East Europeans tend to engage in more routine cases of racist acts than their western peers. They have exhibited it repeatedly, especially during European soccer matches where Black African players from the rich West European clubs tend to be the subject of monkey chants and other racial slurs.

Why this is the case is hard to tell, but I believe that long years of communist rule, and lack of civil liberties and equal right laws in those countries, mixed with misconception and prejudice about the black race may be the main reason. The fundamental difference, though, is that, while most racial discrimination in the rich west is deliberate, prejudice, misconception, ignorance and illiteracy seem to be the main force behind all other forms of racism.

The west is by far the most advanced in every department when it comes to riches, technology, education, civil liberties and, of course, exposure and sensitivity to racial issues. Therefore, it is reasonable to conclude that a westerner who calls a black person a monkey, smelly, and dirty is not doing that out of misconception or ignorance. He or she knows that is not the case. However, a poor illiterate, ill-informed Chinese, South Asian, or Latino, who has been taught since childhood that blacks lives in trees in Africa, that the reason blacks are that color is due to dirt, is definitely harbouring that belief because of his or her illiteracy, ignorance, or misconception and, of course, lack of exposure to a black person.

The truth of the matter is, educated individuals, as most westerners are; know that dirt and smell have nothing to do with skin color. You can be as white as a fleece, but if you don't keep neat and clean, you can be dirty and smelly.

As for my comparison between whites from the east and those of the west, it's a well known fact that countries in Africa were mainly colonized by the Western countries – Britain, Spain, France, Holland, Denmark, Belgium, Germany and Portugal.

Because many western countries have a long history of democracy and civil liberties, millions of blacks were allowed to gain citizenship in these western countries. This led to great exposure between whites and blacks in the west. That has not been the case with most of Eastern Europe, where due to the Iron Curtain; citizens of those countries were not exposed to black people, so they do harbour some long-held misconception about black people.

ELEVEN

Battle Number One - Immigration

October 2004. I had been living in Canada more than two years, when the summons arrived requesting me to appear before the Immigration and Refugee Board. This was the third attempt in as many months to get the hearing for my refugee claim going. The previous two had been postponed because the authorities couldn't find a translator for my Kotokoli dialect. The Refugee Board members wanted to make sure I was what I claimed to be and that I could speak my mother tongue.

The third time is supposed to be lucky. However, I entered the room with a mixture of hope and trepidation but found myself a participant in a very bad comedy. The characters seemed miscast.

First there were the two panel members – the Refugee Protection Officer, a Caucasian male, and a Presiding Judge or Presiding Member of the Board, a female from North Africa. The officer kept repeating his questions to me as if he wanted to be sure and Madam Presiding Member seemed very distracted. Then there was the translator. This time they found one but he didn't understand a word of Kotokoli. Instead, he spoke Hausa, the language of most people in the northern parts of West Africa. I also spoke Hausa, so it should have worked. Think again.

First, my legal representative wasn't happy they didn't have the right translator, but she didn't want the hearing to be postponed for the third time. So, everybody agreed to proceed, with the translator and I conversing in Hausa.

However, right from the start, as soon as this translator tried putting my words into English, he had problems. I spoke better English than him, which the Refugee Protection Officer soon realized. I think he was concerned we were getting nowhere fast so suggested we conduct the hearing completely in English.

I wasn't comfortable with proceeding in English only. I remembered my experience in Germany and it was the Canadian Refugee Board who had demanded the hearing be held in my mother tongue. No way was I taking any chances, so I stood my ground. I was eventually forced to give in after the panel guaranteed that my identity and language would not be an issue as they had enough proof of the former.

However, as the hearing continued, they did become an issue, and the issue took centre stage.

"Are you a Togolese national?" the Refugee Protection Officer asked me.

"Yes," I answered.

"You're sure?" he asked.

"Yes, I'm sure."

"Where are we?" Madame Presiding Member looked around as if she'd just woken from a bad dream.

The RPO brought her back on track while my legal counsel sighed.

The questions, and the interruptions, continued. The RPO and my counsel took turns cluing in Madame.

Unfortunately, the officer at the end rejected my claim. The shocker was when he stood up right afterwards and left the room before my legal representative could present her rebuttal.

Meantime, Madame lived up to her behaviour. In the end, she couldn't make up her mind about how to rule. In most cases, a decision is rendered after the hearing; however, Madame told my counsel and me that she would mail me a written decision.

The surprise with her occurred after the hearing when she told my counsel to return all my files to me. That gave us hope that she might grant my request because if she rejected it, my counsel would need all my files for a Federal Court appeal. My counsel also believed that because Madam was from North Africa and was also a Muslim, she would give me a positive review. However, I wasn't sure she was a Muslim, and if she were, I didn't want any favours because we shared the same religion. I felt I had a genuine case for asylum.

I sought asylum to escape persecution and a possible death sentence which came about from a letter I wrote in October 1994 to a London-based newsmagazine. As a Togolese National who had lived most of my earlier years in Ghana, I had become a staunch opponent of the then Eyadema regime in Togo. My opposition meant I was a target. But at least I was under the protection of the government of Ghana at the time.

My letter changed that. In my letter, I expressed my outrage about Germany's imposed visa restrictions in October 1994 on Togolese nationals traveling to Germany. Until then, it was visa free. My argument was that Germany owes the Togolese people a lot and not only must the visa-free policy continue indefinitely, but Germany must do more to assist Togo financially. My rational was that, because of Germany, Togo lost about a third of its territory to Ghana. In fact, the richest part was lost; its access to the sea was halved. It also lost a share in the biggest river in the region.

I held Germany responsible, because it was their defeat to the English and the French during the First World War that led to Togo losing part of its land and people. This subject is taboo in Ghana, so my letter was seen as a national security threat, although its contents were not meant to harm Ghana. Attempts were made to arrest me. So, I needed asylum.

To make a long story short, while I waited for Madame's verdict to arrive, I pondered my case. I believed it had been mishandled right from the beginning. Madame had been a last-minute replacement for another member who had been around in my other two aborted hearings. This other member was a white female. I was told she had excused herself because she had taken ill at the last minute. I didn't buy that.

I also mulled over the actions of her replacement during the third hearing and some of the cruelties that occurred then.

During this hearing, I had told the panel that I had lived and worked in the Kingdom of Saudi Arabia for more than five years as an undocumented alien. My documents proved it. The North African panel member felt she knew much about the Kingdom and refused to believe that I was able to live in the Kingdom without legal documents. She argued that the Kingdom is a tight-knit society and it was impossible for me to live there, undocumented, as I claimed.

As can be expected, her comments raised questions about my credibility, which by all calculations was unjustified. Anyone familiar with the history of the Kingdom knows that there are always tens of thousands of illegal aliens in the Kingdom and there always would be. The simple reason is because Saudi Arabia is the host and custodian of Islam's two holiest Mosques; it is obliged to receive millions of Muslim pilgrims each year on its soil. Often, many of these pilgrims overstay their pilgrimage visa and hence become undocumented. The Saudi authorities themselves know this phenomenon exists.

Another example, which I found not only childish, but incomprehensible, was the panel's question concerning an attack on me back in my home country. It had to do with a life threatening injury I suffered in a firebomb attack, which by all intent was politically motivated. But despite the clear pictures I submitted as evidence of my injury, the panel refused to believe I was ever hurt because they could not see scars on my face and the other affected areas as shown in the pictures.

I found that offensive and was disgusted they were so callous about my suffering. This bomb attack could potentially have taken my life, yet they didn't show any sympathy for me. While they were assaulting my credibility, they did not realize their own credibility was on the line with such an outrageous statement. For them to take that stand just because they hadn't seen any scar on the affected areas was not only irresponsible, it was against the intelligence of mankind in the highest order. More appalling was they never disputed that the pictures were not of me, or that they were faked. They merely kept hammering at me during the hearing that they could not see any scars.

Of course, when I examine the pictures and the scale of the injury, I realize that it was a miracle I healed without significant scarring; although a closer look at the affected areas shows signs of burns, which my surgeon did later confirm. He was so angry when he heard the board had rejected my injury claim that he gave me a letter to be presented to the Judge at the Federal Appeals Court. The sad scenario was, despite making an issue of my injuries and employing it as one of the reasons to doubt my credibility, the panel never bothered to get a physician or an expert to examine me. They also did not do their own visual inspection of me.

Generally, apart from the luck that led to me healing, it was also apparent my skin color was another reason why the remaining scars aren't visible. But none of that mitigates the panel from suggesting that I was a liar because I had no scars left on my body after a burn. That is the same as calling a person a liar because the person did not die after a serious car accident.

Almost a month after the hearing, Madame's verdict arrived in the mail. She had sided with the Refugee Protection Officer and rejected my claim. Despite my disappointment, I wasn't surprised. As I read her decision, it was clear to me she had not only misunderstood things I had said (perhaps because she was a late replacement), but it was clear she wasn't an expert on my region of origin.

We are constantly told that judges on the panel are well-trained and have immense information about countries they are asked to rule on. In reality, though, that is only half the truth. They may have knowledge about events in various countries, but their information is often limited, which is why they frequently ask questions that are self-explanatory, questions such as "why didn't you report the incident to the police."

It is important to add that the other person on the panel was white. Despite his rejection of my claim, he was very friendly at times, and on all the three occasions that we met, he surprisingly served me water, even though he was in his late sixties. His rejection was candid – he thought my claims couldn't be collaborated; however he thought I was consistent and articulate. That is important, because in most cases inconsistency and lack of credibility are the main reason claims are rejected.

Throughout the years, I have also learned that the judges

and other officials in charge of refugee issues hate being told the truth. I have observed that the more honest and truthful you are, the more it is used against you. I believe this is one of the reasons the panel rejected my claim. They used my previous claim history in Germany to reject my Canadian claim despite the different circumstances leading to the former claim issue. They failed to recognize that in Germany the authorities didn't give me the chance to get my documents.

As already explained, these officials gave me less than two days after I arrived carrying another person's ID to prepare for my hearing. On the day of my hearing I had no single document to prove my identity, so it is logical that they rejected my claim chiefly on that ground.

But when I arrived in Canada I was using my own identity, although I could have lied. I could have changed my identity and also could have told the authorities I had never requested asylum in any other country. Because I told the truth, I was hurt by the panel's doubts about my credibility. My friends in Germany did it and succeeded. When the authorities refused their claims and tried to deport them, they escaped to neighbouring states, changed their names, their ages and identities, and got recognized. I could have done the same when I arrived in Canada especially as Canada is far away from the European Union where member countries have integrated their refugee systems. This integration makes it hard for failed refugee claimants to seek refuge in another member state.

When I arrived in Canada, I was advised to change my identity, especially my name, and also to keep quiet about asking for asylum in another country. However, I refused to take the advice, because I didn't want to lie. I also thought I had a genuine case of asylum, which was unfairly rejected by the German authorities. I had the courage to do it because I believe and trust the Canadian justice system, which for me is one of the best, if not the best, in the whole world. And despite the rejection of my claim by a few individuals, I still believe in the system.

Canada is one of the few countries which has made diversity one of its top priorities. Unfortunately, despite the good intentions of the Canadian government, racism exists big time among people in positions to ensure fair and balanced immigration of people from the four corners of the world. As shown in the tables on pages 132 and 133, Black Africans are the sole losers in the immigration equation.

Obviously this clear case of inequality cannot be blamed on white people, because unlike Germany or elsewhere in the developed world where immigration officers and immigration judges are often all whites, Canada has immigration officers of much diversified background, perhaps the most diversified in the whole world. Therefore, any racism occurring in the Canadian immigration system, as often has been reported in the media, is not just white racism.

As part of its generous policy of diversity and multiculturalism, it is hoped that equality exists in the way immigration officers conduct their business. As Janice Charette, former Deputy Minister of Citizenship and Immigration Canada put it on May 27, 2005, *"Canada's immigration program is found on the principles of fairness, integrity and balance. The process is without reference to ethnicity, religion or country of origin of applicant."*[2] Compared to other developed countries, I couldn't agree more, but as the tables below illustrates, it seems clearly Black Africa is not part of that cherished principle of balance and fairness.

Incidentally, the then Deputy Minister was making those comments in reply to reports from the Vancouver Province. A story in this newspaper had suggested that Canada's immigration system of setting immigration targets for its missions abroad unfairly limited the number of successful applicants from countries such us India. That is very strange indeed, because as the table shows, India is one of the top five source countries, second only to China, in almost all areas – skilled, family, economic and even refugee class. Black Africa, south of the Sahara, despite all its troubles, doesn't even make the top five.

The conventional wisdom is that because Africa is the continent with brutal wars, natural disasters and the most displaced people on earth, its sub-Saharan countries should be among the top five countries, at least in terms of the refugee class. But the table below tells the whole story. The overall number of Africans permitted to land in all cases is just a fraction of the number allowed for one of the top ten countries listed.

Table One- Class of Immigration by Top Ten Source Countries. 2004

Economic Class Country of Last Permanent Residence	%	Family Class Country of Last Permanent Residence	%
1.China 24,509	18.3	1. China 9,026	14.4
2. India 15,230	11.4	2. India 8,860	14.1
3. Philippines 9,053	6.8	3. Pakistan 4,067	6.5
4. Pakistan 5,665	4.2	4. Philippines 3,970	6.3
5. Romania 4,754	3.6	5. United States 3,806	6.1
6. France 4,537	3.4	6.UnitedKingdom 1,822	2.9
7. South Korea 4,475	3.3	7. Vietnam 1,666	2.7
8. Utd. Arab Emirate 4,086	3.1	8. Sri Lanka 1,516	2.4
9.UnitedKingdom 4,013	3.0	9. Jamaica 1,336	2.1
10. Iran 3873	2.9	10. Iran 1064	1.7
Total- Top Ten **80,198**	**60**	**Total- Top Ten** **37,133**	**59.2**
Total-All Others **53,545**	**40**	**Total-All Others** **25,612**	**40.8**

Table 2- Class of Immigration by Top Ten Source Countries. 2004

Refugee Class Country of Last Permanent Residence	%	All Classes Country of Last Permanent Residence	%
1. Pakistan 2,868	8.8	1. China 36,410	15.4
2. Columbia 2,818	8.6	2. India 25,568	10.8
3. China 2,536	7.8	3. Philippines 13,299	5.6
4. Afghanistan 2,239	6.9	4. Pakistan 12,796	5.4
5. Sri Lanka 2,077	6.4	5. United States 7,493	3.2
6. Sudan 1,379	4.2	6.United Kingdom 6,056	2.6
7. Zimbabwe 1,333	4.1	7. Iran 6,063	2.6
8. India 1,180	3.6	8. Romania 5,655	2.4
9.Dem. Rep. Congo 1,119	3.4	9. South Korea 5,337	2.3
10. Somalia 1,084	3.3	10. France 5,027	2.1
Total- Top Ten 18,633	**57.0**	**Total-Top Ten 123,704**	**52**
Total- All Others 14,050	**43.0**	**Total- All others 112,104**	**47.5**

Source: Ministry of Citizenship and Immigration Canada.[3]

Besides the refugee class, the reason often used to justify the low number of sub-Saharan Africans is because of the Federal Skill Workers Program. But apart from stereotype or perhaps racism, which might be the reason, there is absolutely no justification for the disparities. If skills and language proficiency are a requisite for being a landed immigrant, as is the case with the Federal Skill Workers Program, I believe that many landed immigrants from the five top source countries are no more skilful than Black Africans are. I have met and worked with many of these people; many do not speak either of Canada's two official languages.

Canada's point system, which allows prospective immigrants to secure permanent residency, requires applicants to be fluent in one of the official languages, English or French. Some immigrants from these top five source countries also haven't the slightest idea about the skills they claim to have learned.

I found it a common occurrence that some of these so-called skilled workers tried to play catch-up with their declared skills. For example, at one company where I worked, many men claimed to have studied MIG and TIG welding processes, but when asked about the full meaning of the terms, they became flabbergasted and either turned silent or stuttered out an incorrect definition. When asked about welding defects such as porosity, slag inclusion, undercut, etc., they became confused. Yet they claimed to be professionals in several welding processes.

They also struggled in understanding simple instructions on jobs assigned to them. This was so apparent that one of my supervisors used to jokingly ask where and how these guys got their certificates as skilled workers and how they managed to pass their interviews at the Canadian missions abroad. I personally handled so many situations as Tools Room Keeper, where these men came in to borrow a particular material or tool but they had no idea what they were looking for. So, I find it ironic that they have the upper hand over Black Africans who are skilled.

By the way, don't get me wrong. My use of the Canadian example doesn't mean it is the worse system, far from that. If anything, Canada has the best system. It is arguably the most liberal, most humane, and the most flexible immigration system in the world.

The rational for me using it as an example, however, is if this problem exists in Canada, then you can imagine how bad the immigration system is in some other developed countries where the process is very stringent and very anti-black. I must also reiterate that Canada has one of the most diverse immigration officers of any developed world, with officers from every ethnic background. Therefore, it is wrong to assume that white racism is the reason for Black Africans not receiving their fair share in the Canadian Immigration system.

But sometimes you expect some common sense from refugee officials. Take my case. On three occasions, the Board was unable to get a translator who spoke my native Kotokoli language. Because I am fluent in multiple languages, namely, German, English, Arabic, Hausa (the most popular native language in western Africa), Akan (spoken by about 70 per cent of Ghanaians), and of course, my Kotokoli language, there is no question I am a good asset not only for Canada, but to the Board itself. They could have considered using me as an interpreter, especially as their job requires the use of translators, which they often have difficulty finding.

The fact that they struggled to get someone from my tribe or country to act as interpreter shows that I might be one of the few Togolese in the entire country, and perhaps the only Kotokoli person in the province of Ontario, if not the whole country. So, with the government's policy of diversity and multiculturalism, it was very reasonable to expect them to at least have used some discretion and common sense in their decision. They should have considered that federal officials would have already cleared me from being a security threat because that is a requirement of Canadian Immigration Laws for eligibility to refer a case to the Board. Besides, for over two years prior to my hearing, I was working and paying my taxes and was a very good resident who had never had any problems with the law.

In general, Black Africans are historically not known to have links to terrorism, hijacking and high profile hostage-taking cases, yet they are the ones to be subjected to intense scrutiny at ports of entries, refugee hearings, interviews and stringent immigration processes. It reminds me of some events I witnessed in Germany.

While I was at the transit centre and later at the refugee home, we used to have Algerians and Kosovo Albanians who shoplifted regularly at department stores such as Kaufring and Woolworth. This always shocked me because they were never caught.

But the stereotyping and profiling of black people was so rampant, black people tended to catch the attention of the security at every department store they visited. When we told our Algerian and Albanian friends about the whole situation, they did not believe us until one day we planned with some of them who were not necessarily shoplifters to window shop at a few department stores. As we moved from one lane to another and from one store to another, it became clear to them that security stalked the blacks, while the Algerians and Albanians moved freely from one area to another without anyone bothering them.

There was one Algerian who was so sophisticated in how

he conducted his shoplifting; we thought he used some kind of voodoo to blind the storekeepers. This fellow always came home with large quantities of quality stuff to sell to fellow refugees. Sometimes he packed them in two to three big Samsonite suitcases and shipped them out of the country. Considering the scale on which he conducted his business, we wondered why he was never caught despite the plethora of modern-day surveillance technology.

Unfortunately, we couldn't hand him over to the authorities for several reasons, including our own safety. But it is not just in Germany or just a white man stalking us. I have faced similar incidents everywhere I have traveled. I have had East Indians, Arabs, Chinese and Hispanics follow me whenever I enter their shops.

But back in Canada, I attend to my refugee claim with some hope. After the Board's denial, I had no option except to apply for a judicial review with the Federal Court of Appeal. However, while I write this book, the Court's decision is still pending. The sad part about the appeal process is that it is never easy to have the Court overturn the Board's decision. But as a strong believer in the fairness of the Canadian system, I am optimistic that an impartial judge will give me a positive review and overrule the Board.

TWELVE

Battle Number Two - Cancer

My fairy tale life continued on its disaster roll. A month after the Refugee Board denied me asylum, I had to face the unthinkable.

I was at work, taking my lunch break outside the company. It was summer and I was enjoying the fresh warm air. I sat in my routine place under a tree. A Hungarian friend, who was our maintenance manager, had joined me. After our lunch break, I stood up and started back to the work area.

"Ali," the Hungarian said from behind me. "There's something behind your ear, a lump. It looks like it's growing big. You should see a doctor."

I turned around and looked at him. I'd known about this for five months. Then, in May, I had risen one morning and felt around behind my ear and found the spot had swollen a little. However, because I couldn't see it, I thought it was only small and negligible, especially as I felt no pain. But when my Hungarian friend saw it and expressed concern, I moved fast. Maybe it was bigger than I thought. The next day I saw my family physician.

"It's a benign tumor, he said." "But I strongly advise you to get it removed as soon as possible." I just stared at him.

"I'm ordering blood tests, ultra sound and x-ray."

After the tests came back, my doctor referred me to a surgeon at the St. Joseph's Health Centre in Toronto. There, too, I had to undergo a series of tests. At this stage, all the test results had shown the tumor was benign. However, the surgeon scheduled surgery for November 30, 2004 to remove the tumor.

I went into instant panic.

I couldn't face a needle let alone going under the knife. My practice had been to skip visiting my family physicians. Surgery frightened me so much that if I was watching a documentary depicting any surgery, I'd turn off the TV. And now my surgeon was not only booking me for surgery, he described the procedure in minute detail. I was so scared I wrote him a letter and almost refused to have the surgery done.

After the surgeon read my letter, he called me and asked me to come over so that he could clarify things for me.

"It's no big deal," he said, after I had slinked into his office. "We put you right under. You won't be aware of a thing. We'll do everything to minimize any scars. You'll be like brand new."

So, I swallowed my anxieties and fears and consented to the surgery. At 11:00 a.m. on November 30, I reported to St. Joseph's. After their routine admission protocol, I was put to sleep. Then it was 6:00 p.m. and I was being wheeled from recovery to a room where I was told I would spend the night. In my groggy state, rest was all I wanted. And comforting care.

I received the latter from the first nurse, a Caucasian, who was so considerate and friendly, she made me feel at home. She was punctual, whether it was disposing of my urine or coming in to check my condition. She was also very jovial and even sometimes spent a few moments with me. But her shift soon ended and her replacement arrived.

It was like day and night. The replacement, a Hispanic woman, was mean and unfriendly; I wish I had reported her. The first nurse had advised me to call for assistance by pressing an emergency instrument attached to my hand any time I needed help especially if I felt any pain and required pain killers. Nurse number two, however, acted neither promptly nor in a cooperative manner when I called for assistance.

"My urine bottle is full," I said when she finally entered my room. "Could you either dispose of it or give me a new bottle?"

She looked at me as if I had asked her to perform surgery. "Oh, you don't need to pee in a bottle. You can go to the washroom yourself. It's right over there." She pointed to the wash room. "You can walk there." I was in a dilemma. As a shy guy, I didn't like urinating in a bottle in front of an audience.

However, I was in so much pain that just sitting up hurt. It seemed I had no choice. The bathroom it was. But as I struggled to get there and back, I was filled with anger and decided to report her. Back in bed, I changed my mind. The last thing I wanted to do was to put somebody into trouble, especially as I might well be lying in my deathbed. I'd had surgery in a sensitive area of my body – my head, neck and ear – and I was still in pain and didn't know what could happen. As a believer in God, the best thing I could hope for was to forgive my enemy in my final moments, even if the enemy was responsible for my death.

At about 11:00 a.m. that day I was released and took a taxi home. I spent several days recuperating at home. My surgeon made an appointment to remove the stitches and to assess the progress of my overall condition. When I saw him, he had mixed messages for me.

"The good news is you are making progress in healing," he said. "The bad news is the tumor is extended to sensitive areas around your right ear and right eye. So you will need radiation therapy to kill those cells. I'm also sending the removed tumor to Mount Sinai Hospital for further testing."

While I waited for the results, I continued to work, despite the dusty smoky environment that lacked any ventilators. With my immigration status still unresolved, I had no choice.

I received a call from Princess Margaret Hospital, which is also in the same vicinity as Mount Sinai. The Chief Oncologist there told me the final pathology result – a plethora of medical terms. The result was consistent with a basal cell adenocarcinoma; the pathology specimen on the tumor showed extra parenchyma disease with positive resection margins and perineural. My tumor wasn't benign – it was malignant cancer.

Only God knows how devastated I was to hear that news, especially as I have never smoked. Thankfully it was in its early stage and was curable. Having undergone X-ray, MRI, and other processes, I was now scheduled for eight weeks of radiation treatment at the Princess Margaret Hospital, Canada's leading cancer treatment centre.

As it turned out, February 2 to March 29, 2005 became one of the most gruesome and agonizing periods in my life. I faced the pain and side effects of the radiation treatment.

At one point I had to forego eating for two to three consecutive days because I had lost taste for any food on the planet. I also had to stop working, temporarily. I felt very lonely. It was sad to know that there was no one at my side throughout my ordeal. Sometimes I woke up in the night and began to cry. After my treatment, which required some healing time afterwards, I was too ill to go outside my apartment for four or five days. I sat on the couch or lay in bed, stared at the walls and ceiling and asked the unthinkable question.

What happened (God forbid) if I collapsed?

When I look back at the way I was living, there was every possibility I could have been dead in my bed or apartment for days or weeks without anybody knowing.

I did not have many friends in Canada, so I wasn't receiving any telephone calls. Sometimes I went a week or more without receiving a single phone call from within Canada. The only communication I used to have regularly was from my fiancée, Aisha, who was in Ghana.

Unlike Germany, where I had many girlfriends, resulting in a slight bump in my relationship with Aisha, when I arrived in Canada, I promised her "no affairs." We were together before I left Africa and I hadn't seen her since.

My hope has always been to secure permanent residency so that I will be able to bring her to live with me. I have kept that promise. That is why I didn't have a friend by my side during my cancer journey, a journey that continues as I write this book.

My journey reached its scariest level on the tenth day of my treatment. That evening, after my treatment, I experienced a very serious headache. When I woke up in the morning and looked in the mirror, I noticed my eyes were unusually red.

First, I thought I had "arc eye." This is a welding term meaning a person has exposed his naked eyes to bright arc rays or reflected glare. But I had done little welding in the last few weeks.

I dressed and headed for my treatment. As I arrived at the hospital, a nurse, Margaret, saw me and noted my eyes were very red. She questioned me about it, but I couldn't give any possible reason. She quickly reported it to my oncologist. It was later determined that I might be receiving too much radiation. The oncologist ordered the technicians administering the radiation to reprogram my radiation dosage. I did not experience any further serious headache or red eye. But it was a close call and it shows how simple medical errors could be deadly.

Margaret, my case manager and assistant to my oncologist is not only an awesome lady, but a nurse's nurse and of the finest white women I have ever met. During my scheduled thirty-five day radiation treatment, Margaret not only met my oncologist and me every Wednesday in the nurse's room, of the B2 Radiation Unit, she made it her duty to see me almost everyday. Her office is on the second floor, four floors above the B2. In most cases, I would be sitting in the waiting room and Margaret would suddenly appear. She would hold me and comfort me – to the surprise of other staff members, fellow patients and anyone else present. I don't know Margaret's age but I would guess she would be in her mid to late forties, but she was like a mother figure.

She not only provided me with a fine dietician, another Caucasian lady who supplied me special canned food, at no cost to me, Margaret also obtained medication for me, free of charge. Every time I was given a prescription, namely: Neutragel (for the protection of my teeth and gums) and sunscreen lotion to protect the treated area from exposure to the sun, she was there.

"Ali, these medications are very expensive," she said. "Do you have enough money with you?"

"Yes," I replied.

"Ali, wait. I am going to see what I can do. I am surely not going to let you buy that."

She'd leave and reappear within minutes; carrying every medication I had been prescribed.

One day both of us became very emotional. It was during

the latter part of my treatment, and I was beginning to feel the full effect of the radiation. As I was warned at the beginning, the treated area began to peel and I needed to apply salted water and special lotion to prevent permanent damage. In a real world, I needed a second person – a loved one or family member to dress up the area and then apply the necessary medication. This was to be done at least twice a day.

"Do you have someone at home to do this for you? Margaret asked.

"No," I replied. "My fiancée is in far away Ghana.

She began to cry. I cried, too. At that juncture she realized why I was always alone at my treatment even though I had been advised to come with a loved one or a friend to help ease my anxiety and stress. Unfortunately, that was my situation. Absolute loneliness and aloneness.

Margaret took me to a nurse's room, dressed up a bed and asked me to lie on it. As I lay down, she went and got a white napkin, soaked it in salty water and placed it on the affected areas. After a few minutes, Margaret removed the cloth and then applied a special lotion on the treated area. She then told me that I had to do that at least twice a day until the area healed. The treated area would remain sensitive and could not be exposed to sun rays for the rest of my life. Meanwhile, as I dressed to leave, Margaret brought me some more sunscreen lotion, baking soda and other medication.

That wasn't all.

One morning as I was at home and feeling very lonely, my phone rang. I picked it up.

"Hello," I said into the receiver.

"Hi Ali; it's me Stephanie, secretary to your oncologist. May I please have your Canadian government client ID number and name, date of birth and address of your fiancée?"

Her request surprised me. As our conversation continued, I

learned Margaret had lobbied my oncologist to write a letter to the Canadian High Commission in Accra requesting my fiancée be allowed to pay me a visit on humanitarian grounds.

However, the immigration officers at the Commission rejected the application because they figured I was healed and my fiancée's presence wasn't necessary. I was disappointed, but not angry. Of course, after everything I had gone through, I couldn't be cross with anything connected to the Canadian government.

Through their unique and universal health care system I received excellent treatment with the possibility of defeating one of the world's most deadly and scariest diseases. I couldn't have asked for more. I pray that Canadian politicians and Canadian people do everything to keep that cherished health care system which makes Canada unique from the rest of the world. I also hope to have children and to teach them to love a country called Canada.

On the lighter side, though, I am generally a fashion-conscious guy and I have a massive collection of top quality clothing in my closet. Every day I went for my treatment, I wore a different outfit. Margaret would ask me, where the clothing came from? I would smile and bury my hands in my arms. But what a remarkable lady. Margaret's husband, if she has one, must be the luckiest man on earth.

I still didn't know the exact cause of my cancer but was suspicious of my workplace environment. I decided I was not going to go back there after I was healed. During the last week of my sick leave, I drove to the City of Brampton to register with an employment agency. Brampton is a city I had visited only once before and I really didn't know much about it. But based on the ad I saw in the newspaper, the agency was located on Queen Street, which is one of the city's major streets.

After several minutes spent looking for somewhere to park my car, I came across an empty spot at George Street, a few meters away from Queen Street. I parked and got out to put some coins in the nearby parking meter. Just before I began walking towards Queen Street I heard music playing from the direction of my car. I turned around and realized the music was actually coming from my car.

No! No! But it was. I had left my bunch of keys, including my car key, locked inside the car. I kicked the front tire of my car, repeatedly, while cursing myself. I just couldn't believe I had done something so stupid.

As I stood there not knowing what to do, I saw a beautiful black sister with fake curly blond hair. She was yakking on her cell phone while trying to cross from the other side of George Street. I waited as she made her way majestically. She continued with her conversation as she strutted north of Queen Street. I followed her. As soon as I saw her flip her cell phone shut, I approached, greeted her and asked if she could call a tow truck for me so that I could get my car key locked in my car.

"No! No! I am busy. I don't have time," she replied in a Caribbean ascent. She glared at me, then turned and stomped away.

Looking dejected, I approached a Caucasian man stepping down from his truck.

"Good morning, sir," I said. "I have left my car key in the red car parked right there. Can you help me?"

"Oh my God! This must be making you crazy, I guess," he said. "I have had similar problem in New York City and it cost me some time and hundred and fifty bucks. Since then I have always had a second key with me."

"Can you call a tow truck? I don't have coins with me."

"Sorry, I don't have that either."

After some minutes with no hope of assistance, I decided to move on. I could see he genuinely felt my pain and was ready to help in any way he could, but I realized he didn't have an answer for me. So I thanked him and proceeded to the employment agency. It was closed.

Looked like I was locked out of everything.

I started my way back. I saw a young white man standing in front of a beauty shop. He wore an apron and was eating a sandwich.

"Good morning, buddy," I said. "My name is Ali. Do you live around hear?"

"I worked in there." He pointed to the beauty shop.

"Please, I need to make a phone call. I have left my car key in my car and locked it up."

"Come on, follow me."

He led me inside the shop and over to the front desk. Sitting at the desk was a true blond queen.

"Doris, here is Mr. Ali. He needs to use the phone; he has locked up his car key in his car," my new-found friend said to the lady at the desk.

Doris handed me the phone book to search for the operator or whomever I wanted to call. After I found a number, I tried to give it to her to make the call for me but she wanted me to do it myself. I picked up the receiver.

"Wait," she said. "Do you really want to do this? It's going to cost you a lot of money, you know."

"Well I have no choice. I have to face the consequences for my stupidity."

"No. Wait. I am not going to let you do this. I am going to call my insurance company and see what I can do for you." She pulled a card from her purse and dialed. "I have a customer here in my shop who has left his car key locked in his car. I need your help."

The irony was, we had known each other for just a few minutes, and she had no information about me except my name. The fellow at the other end needed some information – my name, the model and color of my car, the license plate, where the car was parked, and whether I had a cell phone so that the operator could contact me when I left the shop. Doris put a paper and pen on the table and wrote all the questions the operator asked and I wrote down my answers for her to relay to the fellow on the line.

Thankfully, the trick worked. But Doris was a bit upset.

"The operator won't be arriving for 30 minutes," she said. "That must be too long a time for you."

"I will wait the whole day if necessary," I replied.

As I left, she gave me her phone number. I thanked her. I felt overwhelmed by her kindness. As I reached the door, I saw her throw her hands in the air.

"I have done one good thing this morning which I am proud of," she said to the ceiling.

I returned to my car. After 30 minutes, a Canadian Automobile Association (CAA) operator arrived right where I stood. I waived as he slowed down. In less than 40 seconds he had opened the passenger door of my car.

"Oh my God, your car stereo is still on," he said.

"Yes." I looked at him. "That is it?"

"That is it."

Before I could ask what drink he preferred because I wanted to give him a tip, he had jumped in his truck, waved at me and taken off. I stood behind my car in amazement.

In some ways I wasn't locked out of life.

PART TWO

MY PERSONAL THINKING (OP ED)

THIRTEEN

Arab Double Standard

For decades, Black Africa has been with the Arab world every step of the way over the latter's grievances with the state of Israel. Whether at the United Nations, Non Align Movement, the former Organization of African Unity (OAU) and the present day African Union (AU), Africans have sided with the Arabs.

Until the early 1990s, when the Middle East peace process seemed possible, the majority of Black African countries had broken off diplomatic relations with the State of Israel, and strictly adhered to their guns, all in solidarity with the Arab world. The cornerstone of this solidarity is Israel's occupation of the lands it seized from the Arabs in the 1967 war and its ensuing practices in the occupied territories, which many have viewed as abuses of human rights.

However, also for decades, two "so called" Arab nations the Sudan and Mauritania have been engaged in racist wars and atrocities aimed at the elimination of black people from their territories.

For years, pundits and politicians outside the region have

characterized the war between the Khartoum government and the southern rebels as a religious war – the so-called Muslim north and Christian south, respectively. But many Black Africans did not buy that. Neither did I. For years I questioned the motive and intentions of the Sudanese regime and I concluded that it was a racist war.

Today, I have been proven right. The horrible, horrible situation in the Sudan region of Darfur, which some governments, such as the United States, have now officially described as genocide, clearly shows that the Khartoum government has operated on a long-term agenda to ethnically cleanse Sudan of black people or make them sub-humans.

Unlike what we have heard about the war with the southern rebels, i.e., that they were attacked because they were Christians, the vast majority of victims of Darfur genocide are predominantly Black Muslims. In effect, what has been occurring in Sudan is not a religious war, but a racist war.

Sadly, during these times the Arab world remained silent and turned a blind eye to all these atrocities. No condemnation, no action. As one of the poorest of the Arab countries, Sudan could not have sustained any sanctions from the Arab countries had they intervened politically and warned Khartoum to stop its racist war against the blacks in its territory.

In August 1994, when Khartoum's dispute with Egypt over the Nile River escalated and Egypt threatened military action, Khartoum backed down. The problem was solved. In Sudan's current case, I am talking about condemnation, and if necessary, economic and political sanctions. That includes expulsion from the Arab League and the Organization of Islamic Countries as well as an appeal to the United Nations for some action.

If this happened, the world would know that Arabs are

genuinely against any kind of oppression, injustice and human rights violations. Unfortunately, it is too late. What has happened in Darfur has become a black eye in Arab history. Even before the Darfur genocide, there were documented reports of Sudanese Arab slavery of blacks. Yet the Arab world did not see that as a serious breach of international norms. It sickens me to see these repeated actions by the successive Sudanese governments and the Janjaweed Arab militias continue amid complete silence from the Arab world.

Ironically, it is not the first time the Arab world has remained mute about Arab League member countries abusing black people.

For many years, Mauritania has persecuted and systematically tried to cleanse its territory of black people. Mauritania also has, on several occasions, deported its own citizens to Senegal and other West African countries. Reason for these deportations? The citizens' skin color.

Below are some events that have occurred in the two countries. These events have affected Black Africans in the two countries and exposed the Arab world's double standard and hypocrisy.

Following the publication of a document called the Manifesto of the Oppressed Negro Mauritanians in April 1986, by African Liberation Forces of Mauritania "FLAM," the then dictator of Mauritania, Ould Taya, ordered the arrest of more than hundred black intellectuals, charging them with various crimes against the state. They were subsequently sentenced to long-term imprisonment in September 1986. Their crime was a noble and reasonable call on all political foes to discuss wide- ranging black grievances and the root cause of injustices perpetuated by the Arabs against the blacks.

As if that were not enough, the following year in October

1987, Taya mounted a massive operation detaining several African personnel in the Mauritanian army. About thirty-five black officers were tried in a kangaroo court and sentenced to twenty years imprisonment with hard labour. Many of their family members were deported. That was after Taya had falsely accused them of an attempted coup d'état against his brutal and racist regime.

By this time, though, he had sped up his racial war against the Black Mauritanians. Several black political activists were tortured and killed. This was followed by perhaps one of the worse crimes against black people in modern history. Between 1989 and 1990, Taya forced the deportation of over 200,000 Black Mauritanians to Senegal and Mali, while several thousands were illegally detained or murdered.

Late 1990 saw the arrest of several blacks throughout Mauritania after the government claimed it had foiled yet another coup attempt planned for November 27 that year. Several dozen blacks were killed in government custody and many were tortured.

Concurrently, thousands of blacks were detained without charge or trial, in what was rumored to be a celebration in advance of the first Iraq war. It is important to note that in 1990, the regimes in Mauritania, Sudan and Yemen staunchly supported Saddam Hussein in his so-called "Mother of all Battles" following his invasion of Kuwait.

Meantime, in the Sudan, black people were systematically deported from the capital, Khartoum, and other northern cities, while the regime gave Ethiopian refugees free residence. Remember what I said in the earlier chapters about how people from the Horn of Africa see themselves as different from Africans south of the Sahara? Here, Ethiopians who are north of the Sahara are preferred over blacks south of the Sahara.

In short, everything black is resented and is marked for systematic destruction. It doesn't matter whether it is black culture or black civilization. Besides all these killings and deportations, there is the brutal case of slavery. It is hard to believe that, in this day and age, regimes are allowed to perpetuate this inhuman and barbaric practice without repercussions. The human rights watchdog, Amnesty International, has documented thousands of cases of slavery in Mauritania.

Even more lethal is that slaves are forcefully armed and put under the Arab-led command. The theatre of operation for these slaves is often in the southern black areas where they massacre and intimidate innocent and horrified blacks. This occurrence is similar to those in the Sudanese region of Darfur.

Under the pretext of self-defence, the government also armed militias from the *Haratines* (Arabicized Africans) who have taken control of expelled black lands. Instead of self-defence, the main purpose for forming these militias was to help fight the Arab war on blacks, sow seeds of hatred and division between free blacks and the black slaves. To me, this is a clear classical case of "divide, conquer and rule." It was also meant to protect the stolen black lands for the Arabs. That was the only way the government could reduce and counter any chance of a united Black African front against the Arabs.

As can be expected, slaves who disobeyed or showed dissent towards violence against the blacks were punished severely.

Slavery itself was abolished in Mauritania on several occasions since independence. The first abolition occurred way back in 1905, then in 1961 and the latest on July 5, 1990. However, as mentioned before, anti-slavery organizations and human rights groups have recorded countless cases of semi- or fulltime slaves kept by Arab Mauritanians. In fact, slavery is so common and open that a Kuwaiti journalist, Mohamed Isa al Qadeeri, wrote in a Kuwaiti newspaper in 1989, *"At the end of my visit to Mauritania, among the gifts given me, which I strongly refused by my Arab friends, was a black slave"*.[4]

Similar stories of modern-day slavery have also been reported regularly in the Sudan.

For the benefit of any doubt, below are findings made by some individuals and organizations about slavery in the Mauritania and Sudan.

The head of state from 1960 to 1978, Mokhtar Ould Daddah, kept slaves behind the presidential palace. The successive military committees which have controlled Mauritania since the coup d'état in July 1978 have fluctuated between "return to tradition" – implying amongst the other aspects, that there would be no relaxation of slavery – and the decree of July, 1980 yet again "abolishing slavery."[5]

Africa Watch, a human rights watchdog, in one of its reports, noted:

Abolishing Slavery which is deeply rooted in Mauritania is a difficult and long term problem. Our criticism is not that Mauritanian government has tried to eradicate slavery and failed, but it has not tried at all. We are not aware of any significant practical steps taken by successive governments to fulfill the important responsibilities Mauritania undertook when it passed laws and ratified international agreements prohibiting slavery. Its persistence is largely explained by the fact that legislative enactments have not been accompanied by initiatives in the economic and social fields.[6]

In their report on the resurgence of slavery, published in Sudan in 1987, Drs. Ushari Mahmoud and Suleiman Baldo wrote:

Since 1986, slavery has returned in force, and is not seen by the perpetrators as illegitimate in the context of the present government war policy. The kidnapping of Dinka children, young girls and women, their subsequent enslavement, their use in the Rizeigat economy and other sphere of life and their exchange for money-all these are facts. The government has full knowledge of them. Indeed, the perpetrators of kidnapping and slavery have its allies in the armed militias.[7]

It must be remembered that this report was made over 15 years ago, long before the scorch earth policies in the Darfur region of Sudan.

Unfortunately, all these atrocities, the discrimination and the slavery, have been going on against the backdrop of laws in both Mauritania and Sudan. Paradoxically, these laws criminalize discrimination against groups or persons because of their race or color. And both countries have ratified the African Charter.

This ratification means that the two countries have committed to *respect the right to enjoy human and civil rights and freedoms without discrimination based on race, ethnic group, color, sex, language, religion, political, or any other opinion, national and social origin, fortune, birth or other status.*[8]

However, as noted in the reports above, black people in these two countries have for decades been the victims of vicious racial discrimination and ethnic cleansing, all committed by successive Arab regimes. Blacks in Mauritania repeatedly were denied passports and identity papers. Some blacks even face arrest for simply requesting identity papers.

The Mauritanian regime has not only oppressed its black people, it denies outrageously that blacks even exist in that country. This was made clear by the country's ex-Dictator Ould Taya in an interview with Jeune Africa News Magazine in 1990.

Here is what he said in that interview: *"Mauritania cannot be in the process of Arabization as it is already an Arab country"*[9]

It is important to add that, despite his many atrocities and anti-black stands, when Taya was deposed from office while he attended the funeral of King Fahd of Saudi Arabia in August 2005, he could not seek asylum in either the Kingdom or with any of his Arab friends. Instead, he shamelessly flew to Gambia, a Black African country and sought refuge there.

As mentioned earlier, the Sudanese attitude towards its black population is no different than that of Mauritania. The British rulers of Sudan kept all development projects centered in the northern part of the country; this trend has been continued and reinforced by the successive Arab-led governments.

The only difference with the Mauritanians is that, during the days of the colonial rule by the French, the southern area of Mauritania was the developed part of the country. But in order to punish the black south and make them poor as well as dependant on the Arab north, development projects were moved to the north. Land reforms laws that were introduced in the 1980s were all to the disadvantage of the blacks. Farm lands of black farmers along the fertile Senegal river were taken over and given to Northern Arabs.

I am continually amazed that the Sudan's and Mauritania's repulsive actions bring no benefits to the Arab cause and I wonder if the countries' rulers even realize this. If anything, their practices have done long-term damage to any grievances Arab people might have. How on earth can Arabs demand justice and respect for Palestinians and other Arab rights while for years they have remained silent about the atrocities and annihilation of black people in the Sudan and Mauritania? Their silence dumbfounds me because the misguided leaders in those countries have often linked these deeds to Arab and Islamic causes.

Yes, like many people, I fully support the Palestinian right for an independent state, living side by side with the state of

Israel. Simply put, I hope this is achieved peacefully sooner rather than later. Unfortunately though, thanks to their silence and inaction, Arab countries have forfeited any moral authority to talk about justice. This is going to haunt them for many years.

This is just part of my long list of grievances against the Arab regimes, especially the rich Gulf States. For years, I have been a staunch supporter of the region and continue to be, particularly of the Saudi royal family. As a Muslim, my main concern is about the security of Islam's two holiest Mosques.

With problems everywhere around the world largely affecting Muslims, the last thing Muslims want are instability and chaos at these holy places, which host millions of overseas pilgrims throughout the year. It is great that no serious act of violence has taken place there. So, I am pleased with the way the Saudi's, as custodians, have handled the two holy Mosques.

As a pro-democracy activist, this might sound strange, but that is the way it is considering the special circumstances that the Kingdom of Saudi Arabia faces. I strongly believe instability in the region could have devastating consequences not only to world economies, but it could also threaten international peace and security. In any case, I hope democracy occurs, at its own pace, in the Kingdom of Saudi Arabia.

When I lived in the Kingdom, I used to have heated debates with my friends about the Kingdom and the royal family. The majority of my friends hated the family so much they strongly backed Saddam Hussein's invasion of Kuwait and hoped that he would invade the Kingdom and other gulf states. Their resentment was not because they wanted democracy. If anything, they were in favour of a theocratic government which would govern only via Islamic law. Their resentment was because they saw greediness on the part of the Saudis and the Saudis' refusal to share the wealth bestowed on the Kingdom with other Muslims, namely, poor Muslim communities in Africa.

Many Muslims believe that the riches of the Kingdom come from the blessings God has bestowed on the Prophet Mohammed and that these riches must be shared among Muslims all over the world. Several Muslims also take this belief a step further – they do not believe they need to have a visa to make pilgrimage to Mecca, and Medina, because again they believe the land is for all Muslims. That is the excuse many have used to stay on and become what the government calls "illegal immigrants," but what many of these people consider their religious and natural right.

I may not agree with the various perspectives held by some Muslims. But I think the rich Arab states have not done enough to help poor Muslim communities (especially Black Africans). Whether it is racism or not, it is clear that for years, the wealthy states have not supported non-Arabs communities as they have with, for example, Palestinians or Afghans.

As a consequence, Black Muslims in Africa have become one of the most illiterate and poor people in the world. Illiteracy among Black Muslims is the highest in sub-Saharan Africa because the majority of Muslim parents are reluctant to send their children to schools which are largely Christian-based and because they fear conversion. Yet, the rich Muslim countries have done nothing to build Islamic schools of higher learning in these regions.

Let's look at these missionary-funded or public schools, which constitute over 90 per cent of African state schools. And let's be upfront. Thanks to my mother, I was enrolled in one of the Roman Catholic schools, but still remained Muslim. In all of them, regardless of the students' religious affiliation, they have to say the Lord's Prayer and do Bible studies. (I have no problem with this setup). And it's all due to the efforts of

Christian missionaries. Most of the schools began as missionary before they became public schools. Now let's consider the Arab side.

With the abundance of resources God bestowed on the rich Islamic states, Muslims expected the rich Arab states to do the same for the Black Muslim communities in the sub-region as did the Christian missionaries from the west. But this never happened.

Instead, Black Muslims have seen neglect of their plight, while a lot of money was invested in war zones, such as Afghanistan and other parts in the Middle East, and conflict zones. Anyone who has visited or knows about the region understands what I am talking about. Muslim communities often are found in crowded slums in areas often referred to as *Zongos.* At every train station, bus station and airport, the vast majority of potters and panhandlers are Muslim men, women and children.

A huge difference also exists in the human-to-human relationship between the European missionaries and their Arab counterparts. The Christian missionaries know how to interact with the local Africans. They do so passionately and convincingly by going to villages and remote areas to meet church members and others they might want to convert. However, you rarely see an Arab Muslim scholar do the same.

The stories of Mother Theresa and Lady Diana are typical examples. Even Bill and Melinda Gates, the world's richest couple, and the man I call the greatest man of his generation, have the passion to make similar humanitarian undertakings, intermingling with the poorest of the poorest. Like many missionaries, they are able to go to remote areas in Africa, kiss, hug, hold and comfort the poor, the sick and the downtrodden.

But never in my life have I seen or heard of an Arab sheik,

Prince or Imam, visiting a village to interact with poor Muslims.

I remember very well during my primary school days how Roman Catholic fathers used to treat their church members, especially the youth. Their demeanour and body language were so touching; they could easily get one to convert. And Muslim parents feared this, so many refused to send their children to non-Islamic schools; hence, the huge amount of illiteracy and poverty among Black African Muslims.

Don't get me wrong, I am not talking about building pure Islamic schools or Taliban-like Madrassa'. What I'm talking about is funding and building schools that are secular, but with a visible Islamic identity and Islamic values so that Muslim parents do not have ill feelings sending their children to schools that are run similar to the Roman Catholic and public schools.

Unfortunately, Black Muslims have only seen a constant repeat of indifference and lack of concern with their cause. They see this lack of concern in the Sheiks and Princess overspending their wealth unnecessarily. A case in point is Saudi Prince Al Walid, whose donation of $10 million to the 9/11disaster relief was rejected and was snubbed by the Americans.

Like many of his comrades, he wanted to show off, but it backfired in his face. Instead of donating to the already rich, had he donated that money to a poor Muslim community in Africa to build a school or a health centre, only God would know the rewards and blessing he would receive. Personal humility doesn't fit in with lording it over everyone else.

Besides building schools, the Christians Missionaries have massively funded hospitals and clinics. Everywhere you go in the West Africa sub-region, it is St. Michael's, St Joseph's, St. Peter's Hospital, etc. You will never see Imam, Sheik Khalid's, or Prince Abdullah's Hospitals. That is the way it is, despite Black Muslims being one of the largest religious groups in that part of the world. I often wonder how Muslims have managed to remain resilient and avoid all those temptations and enticements to convert, when you consider the aggressive missionary activities in the region and the lack of support from the rich Arab nations.

The simple truth is the rich Arab states just don't care about what Black African Muslims are going through, whether they are converted or not. Yet these Arab states and their people have the audacity to bill themselves as the guides of the Islamic religion. And that is where it hurts the most. Although Black Muslims do not get substantial help from the rich Arab states, they become victims of everything Arabs do – whether it is terrorism, beheadings, declaring holy wars, issuing religious edits, provoking conflicts, or calling for the destruction of Israel.

The Arabs behave as if they have a monopoly over the Islamic religion, even though the Prophet made his position clear. Every time there is a problem, they go about attacking non-Muslims and ignore the fact that millions of Muslims live as minorities in several countries and those Muslims can also be victims of revenge attacks.

In today's world, post 9/11, Muslims everywhere, regardless of their background and ethnicity, have become subjects of persecution. It doesn't matter whether one is a Black Muslim, White Muslim or Brown Muslim. These persecutions are all due to events in the Middle East where every mad man or ill-informed groups with grievances against the west use Islam and Muslims as an excuse for their nefarious activities.

Another instance showing insensitivity and lack of help by the rich Arab states manifested itself in the wake of the Boxing

Day 2004 Tsunami disaster. The disaster affected millions of Muslims living in Indonesia, but drew lukewarm response from the rich Arab states. The result was not surprising – it added more fuel for some Christian Fundamentalist and anti-Islam forces to continue their vitriol against Muslims and Islam.

My other concern is the refusal by some states in that region to allow women to vote. I have looked for every rational reason possible to understand why woman can't vote and still haven't found one. I lived in the Kingdom for more than five years and accept a number of laws that were in place, such as the partitioning of public buses to separate women from men.

Although it has been widely criticized, I feel it is good if it is for the security of the women when you consider the aggressiveness of some Arab men in the vicinity of women.

It may surprise some readers that I support this. However, because similar steps are being considered in Japan because of incidents of men groping and fondling women in buses and trains, I would not be surprised if other countries, namely, democratic ones, follow suit. However, I don't understand why women should be prohibited from voting. If there is the fear of women being in the same queue as men, separate lines and polling booths could be prepared for them.

Personally, I believe the restrictions are unnecessary, unwise and give these countries and Muslims unwarranted publicity, as well as reinforcing accusations by enemies of Islam that it discriminates against women. My belief is that either nobody votes if these regimes choose not to become democratic and have elections, as that is their prerogative, or everyone is allowed to vote regardless of their race, gender, color or creed.

FOURTEEN

Discrimination – Black American Style

Growing up as a young Black African in West Africa, I was always fascinated with everything African American-their culture, creativity and of course their music. Afro Americans we used to call them. I have always had passionate sympathy for their cause, whether it is their fight for equal rights, equal opportunity or economic justice. But I didn't know that they have some hostility towards Black Africans.

Unfortunately, as my obsession with African American culture and their struggles continued, friends and brothers from Ghana, who had been in the States, returned with a very different view.

They complained bitterly about the African American arrogance and discrimination towards Black Africans. According to our brothers, the African Americans had even given them nicknames such as "JJC" (Johnny Just Come) to refer to new African arrivals.

Because of what was described as inhospitable behaviour on the part of some black immigration officers, prospective travelers to the United States were advised to avoid immigration counters with black officers on duty. According to our brothers and friends, black officers are often strict on Black Africans. In some cases, Africans depend on false travel documents due to visa restrictions. Black officers were considered the ones most likely to identify their brethren with false documents, causing their arrest, detention and deportation.

When I arrived in Germany, I discovered firsthand what my friends and brothers had been talking about. During my stay in that country, I met many African Americans, some of them U.S. Soldiers, in various clubs. Not only were they arrogant and stubborn; they were also heavily involved in their own vicious form of discrimination against Black Africans.

Before my first outing to a club, my friends warned me to be aware of the African Americans because of what they termed their derogatory remarks towards Black Africans and their constant attempt to steal their German girlfriends away from them via smear campaigns.

The African Americans always wanted to let the German girls know the difference between them and the Black Africans. However, we often dressed in similar fashion, so it was difficult for the Germans to distinguish us from them. The Americans believed that might be why the German girls were falling in love with us. For that reason, every time we met in a club, the African American fellows tried every trick to tell the ladies the difference between them and us.

After countless minor encounters, my beautiful young German blond, Melanie and I saw this viciousness first hand. We went to a club often frequented by African Americans. They used to organize the concert shows at the club and always had a heavy presence there. By the time Melanie and I arrived, events were in full swing.

After hanging around for a few minutes, my baby and I

joined the dancers on the dance floor. We did our own thing for nearly an hour, then we decided to take a break and have a drink. We ordered soft drinks and took our seats. As soon as we sat down, I excused myself to visit the washroom. When I returned a few minutes later, I found my baby looking very upset and almost in tears.

"What's wrong?" I asked.

"Nothing," she said. "Let's leave."

"We've only been here a couple of hours?" I took her hand.

"Come on, baby, tell me what's wrong?"

"Nothing," she said. "I just want to leave. Look, I've had a long day and I'm tired."

"Okay. Okay. We'll go."

She was so hurt; she refused to tell me anything until we arrived home. It was only after we had showered and were about to go to bed that she opened up.

"Ali, I don't understand how some people behave so foolishly and irrationally without showing any kind of remorse."

"What do you mean?"

"Ali, as soon as you left, an African American guy approached me and asked to dance. I refused, but he sat down beside me and said some nasty things. He asked me whether I knew you were an African from the jungle and a refugee. I told him, *'Egal'* (It doesn't matter.) He then went on to make further derogatory remarks about Black Africans. At that point my blood started to boil and I warned him I'd slap him if he didn't leave. Fortunately, he had enough sense to see that if he stayed and continued to mouth off, things would get uglier. So he got up and left."

That was the pattern. These guys always had something bad to say about Black Africans, in an attempt to either discourage the German girls from falling in love with us or to let them succeed in snatching our girlfriends away from us. They told the German ladies the only reason we married them was for convenience and to secure a legal residence permit. They called us "jungle people" and said we lived in trees and played with monkeys back in Africa.

It was hard to understand where this jealousy and nastiness originated. However, they failed to realize that the Germans were well aware of their dirty tricks and didn't care a bit about the malicious things they said about us. The German ladies preferred us to them and harboured much resentfulness towards African Americans.

Not only were the German women angry over the condescending remarks the Black Americans kept making about Black Africans, they also concluded that African Americans were very abusive and arrogant. This latter goes back in history to the Cold War when the United States had numerous military bases in Germany, so many Black Americans met and married German women and had children with them. But the relationships weren't all that rosy, my friends and I learned from the Germans. For years, the German women complained of spousal abuse by the Americans.

Over time, the ladies realized the difference between Black Africans and Black Americans and concluded that we were sober, respectful, and loving as opposed to the naughty haughty ways of the African Americans.

The reason for this, though, was simple. The Africans were mostly refugees, and in most cases had to marry German women to secure permanent residence permits. Despite their sober nature, Africans tended to show a lot of respect and love in order to get what they wanted. (And I guess the Black Americans were right about us in this respect.) Black Africans also faced the possibility of imprisonment and deportation in case of spousal abuse, etc., so they were always very careful and generally treated their German spouses with the respect they deserved.

On the other hand, African Americans didn't care, because they didn't face the possibility of being deported to a poor Third World country for any callous behaviour with their German spouses. In the worse case scenario they were redeployed or sent back to the United States, which didn't upset them. In fact, not all the soldiers in Germany are content with their situation; when they do something stupid which could lead to their redeployment to the U.S., it lifts their spirits. I am not saying they do this deliberately to get redeployed, but they are glad to be sent back home.

In any case, the German ladies had learned their lessons first hand about African Americans. Now they were sophisticated and could decide who to give their love to. So whatever nonsense our brothers from America said about us meant nothing to them, as long as they received the love, respect and dignity from us that they deserved.

Although the attempt by African Americans to dehumanize Africans might be shocking, it should surprise no one.

Many African American hit movies contain irresponsible and condescending remarks made by African Americans. Watch such movies as "Coming to America" and "Barbershop" and decide for yourself. Also countless obscene remarks and racial slurs about Africans have been made by Black American comedians and entertainers.

Unfortunately, while these entertainers make people laugh, they fail to realize that hate is no joke and must not be condoned under any circumstances. Telling ethnic jokes and making racial slurs, whatever the purpose, is not a laughing matter. These slurs go to the root of racism and hate. They must be condemned in the strongest terms possible by all rational human beings, especially by people who are one of mankind's most discriminated and humiliated.

God save us, if people who claim to be victims of racial discrimination think they can make racist and hurtful comments about others without consequence. Individuals must be held accountable for their actions. Imagine if a white person made derogatory remarks against African Americans in a movie or on TV, hell would break loose and there would be calls for that person's head. These are part of my long list of grievances with Black America.

Throughout history, every race in their respected Diaspora, has staunchly supported and lent a helping hand to their suffering brethren, politically, economically and morally. The Irish Americans have helped their brethren in Ireland. The Jewish Americans have helped their brethren in Israel proper. The Italians, the Germans, the Polish, etc. have done the same for theirs in their mother countries. Black America needs to wake up too, and help their brethren in Africa. Africa has so many problems, but much of it can be fixed with awareness and awakening.

For example, why hasn't anyone taken the Swiss and other European banks to task for accepting monies looted from poor African people by their corrupt leaders? If banks and companies can be punished or admonished for their links with Nazis and terrorist, why can't the same actions be taken now against assisted theft by the Swiss and others? Is it because the victims are blacks so therefore it doesn't matter? Why are we letting history repeat itself when something can be done – particularly when it is happening to people who need every penny they can get?

Unfortunately, not only have Black Americans distanced themselves from their beleaguered and battered brethren in

Africa, I believe that their attitudes and short sightedness are leading them to self-destruction.

For years I predicted that African Americans would lose their status as the largest minority group in the United States (Hispanics have now surpassed them in this category). Now they are also in danger of being overtaken by the Asian Americans as the second largest minority group.

There are so many reasons for that. If you look at the situation in our world today, with the exception of Africa, every continent has mutual visa-wavering programs. The European Union countries have visa-free programs with the United States and Canada. Australia has a similar program with these countries. The Japanese and the South Koreans also have comparable programs with most of the European Union states and Canada and the Unites States. And even where no visa-wavering programs exist, the issuance of visas is not as strict as it is on Black Africans.

The bottom line is that this lack of opportunity for Black Africans to immigrate as easily as people of other races is bound to decrease the growth of the African American population. And not only does this affect the balance of power from the African American perspective, it has every possibility of eroding the limited influence they might have on issues which their forefathers struggled to achieve.

As mentioned above, it is well known that nearly every race helps their own seek the American dream. The Chinese, Jews, Hispanics, East Indians have done it through solidarity and lobbying to obtain favorable immigration laws for their people. Some have also done it through adoption, etc.

However, you hardly ever hear that rich African American families have adopted Black Africans or helped them immigrate to the United States. If anything, it is White America that normally adopts and helps Africans, mostly through missionary activities. It is also common knowledge that the Mexicans have a history of helping their brethren to immigrate to the United States.

The irony here is that the most displaced people on earth come from Africa; yet they are the ones mostly likely to be denied a visa or have their asylum request randomly refused.

Let's look at Cuban versus Haitian immigration to the United States. Most Cubans aren't black. They have easy entry to the U.S. and generally get automatic residence permits once they set foot on American soil. Haitians, who are predominantly blacks, are returned to their homeland.

However, Black America usually only pays minimal lip service as a protest or doesn't seem to care at all. The only reason to explain this lack of interest is because Haitians are poor refugees, which is an anathema to African Americans. These are some of the colossal failures of Black America. It thinks of itself and no one else. It thinks it is superior to non-American blacks and feels ashamed being linked with them elsewhere. Yet, when public figures from anywhere exhibit racism towards them, they take it personally. Consider the following incident.

When on May 13, 2004, Mexican President Vicente Fox stunned the world by his outrageous and racist remarks that Mexicans were doing jobs which even blacks wouldn't do, the black leadership in America went ballistic and moved heaven and earth to try to get Fox to apologize.

It is important to mention that I wasn't surprised at all that the Mexican president made those remarks, because from my experience with most Latinos or Hispanics, that is their mindset. They whole-heartedly believe they are superior to black people. I have encountered this belief.

One day I sat in a waiting room at a Canadian Human Resources office in Toronto. Also in the room were a

Hispanic woman and her little baby daughter who was causing all sorts of problems, running here and there. Whenever the mother tried to restrain her, she began to cry. To get the baby to stop crying, the lady held me up as a monster to try to scare the baby if she didn't quit crying.

For several minutes the mother pointed at me as soon as her daughter started crying or throwing things around. Once she accompanied her pointing with gestures – she frowned; opened her mouth and bared her teeth in a growl, then stretched her arms and curled her fingers imitating a lion ready to attack.

That was exactly what I understood President Fox to mean by his statement. He believed his people should be commended and not vilified by anti-immigrant groups in the United States because they do jobs inferior black people won't do. The fact that the Mexican population never protested, but instead appeared to have endorsed their president's clearly racist statements, confirms what I have been talking about.

However, the swiftness of Black America's response is the complete opposite to their reaction to prominent individuals' derogatory comments about Black Africans, and black people, in general. Here, the Black American community ignores them. A typical example is the following outrageous statement made by former Mayor of Toronto, Mel Lastman.

"What the hell do I want to go to a place like Mombassa? I just see myself in a pot of boiling water with all these natives dancing around me." He added that he and his wife were afraid of snakes. Strangely enough, he made those comments before leaving on a trip to Africa to garner support from African delegates for Toronto's bid to host the 2008 summer Olympics.

Not surprisingly, the city lost, although I personally had hoped Toronto (which is my favourite city) would win. The unfortunate thing is, those comments came from a Jewish person, whose ethnic group, like the Blacks, has been a victim of racism for centuries.

In another high profile case, Lennart Johansson, the Swedish head of the European Soccer's governing body, UEFA, was quoted by the Swedish newspaper Aftonbladet as making the following racist comments.

"When I arrived in South Africa, the whole room was full with Blackies and it gets damned dark when they're sitting together." The paper further quoted him as adding, *"If they are also angry, then it's not so damned merry."*[10] He later made a public apology.

Incidentally, like Mayor Lastman, Johansson was also in Africa to seek the support of African delegates as he was attempting to beat the rival candidate, Sett Blatter, to become president of the world Soccer governing body, FIFA. Both these scenarios illustrate the contempt many people of other races have for Blacks. If not contempt, what on earth were they thinking when they decided to make those comments at the same time they were seeking the support of Black Africans?

Although the two incidents received widespread condemnation and led to unsuccessful bids by both parties, I was not pleased that those two were not forced out of their jobs as punishment for their racial slurs. I was so furious I was forced to write to some news organizations in London to express my disgust. Following is one of my letters in reaction to Lennart Johansson, the UEFA president.

LETTER

To:
The Editor, West Africa Magazine
43-45 Coldharbour Lane,
Camberwell, London SE5 9NR.

Dear Sir/Madam, *January 1, 1998*

Kindly allow me space in your news magazine to react to recent claims by the UEFA President Lennart Johansson, that he has the support of both African and Asian Football Associations in his bid to succeed Jao Havelenge as FIFA president. If those claims are true, I think posterity would never forgive our brethren in these associations who are said to support his aspirations. The fact is, here is a man who is guilty of having used racial slur against black people and have in no uncertain terms admitted his guilt. But admission of guilt and even an apology alone is not enough. It is just too extraordinary and highly irresponsible for a top official of the sport to be caught in the act, at the time the game is desperately struggling to rid itself of racism.

Personally, I think this man should have been forced out from his current, let alone allowing him to stand as FIFA president. It is sad that, our brethren in most positions of influence continued to suffer this old age disease of inferiority complex. Unfortunately it is the combination of this and their lack of sensitivity to high profile issues such as the above , that has given some people the impression that, they can mess with black people and get away with it. Soccer matches can be organized in order to fight racism and even proceeds given to the Africans as it is seen in recent times, but the fact is, all these efforts would come to nothing if we continue to have top officials of the game who are themselves racist or decline to take tough stand against perpetuators of racism in the game.

Take for example an incident which took place in late 1995. A protest was lodged with UEFA, over racist abuse made against black players in the Ajax Amsterdam team. This occurred during their

Champions League match against a Hungarian club. Surprisingly, no action was taking, and to show their frustration and displeasure with UEFA, the Dutch officials took matters into their own hands, by denying the Hungarian fans visas in the return match in Amsterdam. This is against the backdrop of chilling reports and complaint of racism by Africa's professional soccer players.

Of course, it's not an easy thing arresting individuals who engage in racist behaviors during football matches, but the fact is, if clubs can be punished because of violence perpetuated by their supporters, then the same rules can be applied to clubs whose fans engage in racist abuses. Etc.

Finally, I would like to appeal to all black people across the globe especially those in positions of influence to emulate the examples of the world Jewish congress. Similarly, strong signal must be sent to Mr. Johansen and his like that, the civilized world can not tolerate comments or behaviors such as his, whether they are meant to be jokes or whatever.

Thanks for the space provided.

Mohammed Ali

Klein Koetz, Germany.

What amazes me though is, despite all the international outrage and condemnations nothing positive was heard from the African Americans and its leadership. And I guess the only reason was because the remarks appeared to have targeted Black Africans. But while I breathed a sigh of relief that Johansson was not elected, unfortunately, nearly ten years later, racist incidents in European soccer have more than doubled.

This is where the problem lies – Black America thinks only of itself. But Black is black no matter how Black America wants its skin or hair to look like and no matter how differently they may see themselves from Black Africa. Black Americans must understand that, no matter where they live, no matter what their privileges, no matter what their economic status, no matter how they change their appearance, they still would be called "black," and what affects blacks everywhere affects Black Americans, too.

I keep asking myself the following questions:

Where are the black leaders in America?

Where is the so-called Congressional Black caucus? This is an issue that concerns human dignity.

Why can't they get involved and get European politicians to take the issue seriously the way terrorism is being taken seriously?

Jewish people in America do not utter comments against their brothers and sisters in Israel. American Arabs do not make racist remarks against Arabs in the Middle East. The Chinese, the Indians, Hispanics, etc. take care of their own and do all in their power to raise awareness of their sufferings and grievances. They don't make movies mocking their own brethren; they don't make condescending comments belittling their own people. That is the kind of solidarity Black Africans expect from their brethren in the Diaspora who are in a better position to make their grievances heard by the international community.

Let's put it this way. Let's assume that Africa is as rich and developed a continent as Western Europe or North America. Let's assume that Black Africans do not travel to rich countries performing an endless variety of nasty jobs, and suffering all kinds of humiliation, which are elements of illegal immigration.

If these assumptions were reality, don't you think that Blacks every where would be respected and treated as equals by people of other races? I have no doubt in my mind that the only reason Africans, and blacks for that matter, are disrespected and looked down upon is because of the troubled news and images that are often synonymous with Black Africa – the images of hunger, disease, war, extreme poverty and, of course, illegal immigration.

Now let's get back to reality.

Africa is rich in both minerals and human resources. Did you know that Africa is one of the wealthiest continents in the world in terms of natural resources? If these resources were properly exploited and cleverly managed, the outcome could change the face of Africa in a very positive way. Black people everywhere would feel proud and happy and want to go back home. I have no doubt in my mind that if Africa had been rich and developed like Western Europe or North America, many Black Americans would have intensified the search for their ancestral homes and would claim citizenship in many countries in Africa.

I am not naïve about the difficulties Black America faces in the United States, as it struggles to have its own problems solved. Only a fool would deny that. I am fully aware of how the right-wingers and neo-conservative movements in the U.S. have tried to frustrate Black Americans' struggles for equal rights and civil liberties.

However, I believe the opposition to any grievance about Africa would be welcome even by the most hawkish of the American policymakers who are often uncomfortable with Black American demands. For decades, extremist right wingers in the States opposed genuine black grievances and even supported the then apartheid regime of South Africa. But the world has changed. Most of those who supported apartheid and insisted that Nelson Mandela be jailed forever were the ones who gave him the most standing ovations when, as President of South Africa, he addressed the joint session of the United States Congress.

A lot of these extremists now acknowledge they were on the wrong side of history and have repented. Simply put, some of these people have made a swift "U" turn and would not be as obstructive as they were during the apartheid days if African

Americans had the guts to raise the issue. And trust me, once Africa is rich and developed, it will welcome Black Americans with open arms.

In the final analysis, I believe there are many actions Black America can take to help raise awareness and lobby to put some of Black Africa's issues on the international stage. For instance, countries would not be able to sustain the policy of receiving looted monies from corrupt African leaders if they are put on notice and knew there would be consequences for their actions. Countries would not sell arms to poor countries in Africa. Corrupt African leaders would desist from brutal rule and mismanagement of their people's economies.

Besides consciousness and awareness, Black America can set an example. Black America can use its influence to lobby its own government and other rich countries, especially the group of seven industrialized countries. After all, Africa was colonized by more than half of the countries in this rich club. These countries therefore have moral responsibilities towards Africa

To see if Africa can be a success story or if it is merely a continent doomed to failure, let's take one country, Togo, as an example. First let's give Togo a credible democratic government with an impeccable leadership installed, and forgive all its foreign debt. Let the seven industrialized countries, supervised by the United Nations, put massive investment in place in Togo. Let's free the movement of its goods and people, with the approval of the rich industrialized countries. Give Togo a modern constitution which respects all basic human rights and allows it to buy only defensive arms, the budget of which must not exceed one percent of the country's gross domestic product, approved. The international community will guarantee Togo's security, safety and borders. International watchdogs will check all forms of corruption and mismanagement that occur to make sure there is responsibility, accountability, and of course, severe consequences for any violations.

I bet that this would be a success story and become a perfect example of African renaissance. This is not impossible. With careful planning and seriousness, it is achievable. After all, this is the same plan the Bush administration claims to have for the Middle East. It has been done successfully in Germany and Japan, so why not Africa? It will surely lead to a chain reaction and force the rest of the continent to follow suit. In this case, it can be done without going to war. Imagine, how Africa would be like, if one or two established democratic countries in the continent are invested with the war money slotted for Iraq.

The bottom line is, until Africa is helped to rise from its misery and achieves economic and industrial growth, and political stability, like the rest of the developed world, blacks everywhere on the planet, including African Americans, will continue to be looked down upon by people of other races, those who believe the inferiority of the black intellect is the reason for their backwardness. Needless to say, it is in the high interest of Black America to wake up from its slumber, stop its own form of discrimination against its African brothers, stop its own racism against Indians, Chinese, and whites, etc. and make the cause of Black Africa their own.

FIFTEEN

La Francophonie and Commonwealth

No doubt most of Africa's problems are due to colonialism. I know many people will dispute this fact. However, nobody can claim Africans would not have been able to take care of themselves had they not been colonized, indoctrinated and had their treasures looted. Like the saying goes, you break it; you fix it.

The analogy I am trying to draw here is because the colonial masters took it upon themselves to colonize Africa; they are responsible for whatever is wrong with Africa today.

Many bad actions that are responsible for Africa's troubles happened then and continue to this day. These include: redrawing the continent's borders, causing some countries to lose territory, leading to border wars with devastating consequences; forcing tribal groups who normally don't like each other into one entity, leaving lasting conflict on the continent; systematic looting of the continent's precious treasures; enforcing the policy of divide and rule, pitting African against African; supporting African despots who looted the country's money and deposited it in European banks, not to mention the brutal rule those despots inflicted on their people.

This is why it hurts, when today I hear politicians in the

developed world, especially in those countries that colonized Africa; try to use immigration as the platform for their political ambitions. Africans, in particular, have been targets of stringent immigration laws with xenophobic politicians accusing them of being economic refugees, etc. Africans could receive help from their African American brethren.

It is fair to say that the holocaust would not have been taken seriously except for the influence of the powerful Jewish lobby in the United States. The payment of compensation to the holocaust survivors and punishment of the Swiss and German banks and companies would not have happened without the powerful pressure initiated by Jews in the Diaspora.

As a matter of fact, the security and survival of the Jewish state of Israel would be in serious trouble if it weren't for the good work of the World Jewish Congress and other Jewish organizations in the Diaspora. On the other hand, Black America has no such link. Bill and Melinda Gates, Bob Geldof, Bono, and George Clooney, are perfect examples. I know Oprah Winfrey has started making some movements, which is a step in the right direction, albeit long overdue.

But again look at the celebrities leading the way; Angelina Jolie, Brad Pitt, Madonna – all whites. If you take the current situation in Darfur where black people are being slaughtered like animals, the people in the centre stage fighting to call international attentions are mainly whites.

Not only do Black Africans deserve easy immigration passage to most countries which colonized them, they also deserve restitution from these countries and automatic honorary citizenship.

That is why I don't understand why African countries are in organizations, such as La Francophonie, which are linked to colonialism. La Francophonie (Francophone in English) was originally created exclusively for all former French colonies and the colonial master, France. This also means the official language of those countries is French.

However, in the last few years, France wanted to increase its sphere of influence and to rival the much larger British Commonwealth. So France invited countries which it had never colonized or linked with.

More than 10 countries on Africa's west coast are French-speaking and members of Francophone. However, not all this organization's countries are French-speaking, for example Egypt and Zimbabwe. Zimbabwe joined after it was suspended from the British Commonwealth because of its human rights violations. Ironically, most member countries in these two organizations have serious human rights violations.

It is hard to imagine that, after all these years, there is no single organization which links African Americans and their brethren in Africa, while the British Commonwealth and Francophone still exist. That is a shame. These two organizations are symbols of colonialism and imperialism, which I strongly believe perpetuated Africa's holocaust, period. Think about it and then think of Germany forming and heading an organization for all the countries it occupied and ruled from 1933 to 1945.

Only God knows all the details of what the colonial masters – for example, Portuguese arriving in Ghana in 1471 and British taking over from 1621 to 1956 – did to Africans. The general consensus is for centuries they ruled Africans, brutalized them and sent them on treacherous roads of slavery. No television cameras or graphic images existed to prove any atrocities, lootings, killings, etc. But there is no doubt about what happened.

The colonial masters also fought and took control of ancestral lands of Africans, until the latter fought back and won independence. A typical example is the sad case of the Ashanti people of Ghana and their capital city, Kumasi, which is also the second capital city of Ghana.

The British repeatedly invaded the Ashantis and the city. First in 1874, the British, under the leadership of Major General Sir Garnet Wolseley and his expeditionary force, invaded the Ashantis, in Ghana's interior, and entered Kumasi. After a brutal war in the jungles, the British captured it. This is when the British were said to have found the city empty.

In 1895, the British again sent another expeditionary force against the Ashantis. This time the leader was Colonel Sir Francis Scott. Once again British troops entered Kumasi and forced the Ashantis into a protectorate. However, when their King, Prempeh, refused the British demand to pay 50,000 ounces of gold, he and his immediate family members were taken prisoner and exiled to Seychelles, another country. King Prempeh was returned from exile in 1925.

It is important to note that, at the time, the British had the Fantis on their side. The Fantis occupy Ghana's coastal and central regions and are archenemies of the Ashantis. The Fantis were middlemen in the slave trade. Fantis, like the Ashantis, are also part of the Akan tribe in Ghana. Akans make up about 50 percent of Ghana's population. The British have also conquered other native groups further north of the Ashanti.[11]

Many of these wars between the British and the Ashantis occurred because the British attempted to steal the golden stool. This stool is made of pure gold and is a very powerful symbol of the Ashanti Kingdom.

History has it that the stool was conjured from the skies by a powerful fetish priest named Komfo Anokye, a good friend of one of the Ashanti kings. Anokye was said to have presented it to the Ashantis and endowed it with magical powers to help the Ashantis fight their wars. Many believe the stool is the reason the Ashantis were very strong and why they managed to defeat the almighty British army in some of their wars.

It is true that the forefathers of Africans were also used to fight for their colonial masters, which might have contributed to the colonizers' successes in winning their wars. In turn, this enhanced their power and influence and led to wealth and stability for these countries. I think this alone should be the reason for automatic citizenry of Africans, today.

However, as the children and grandchildren of these brave men and women try to reap the benefits of their ancestors, they are called many derogatory names such as criminals, lawbreakers, and economic refugees. The doors to Britain, France, Germany, Holland, Portugal, Spain and Belgium are being shut in their faces.

Before the British arrived, Ghana was made up of several different kingdoms. The British put it together and named it Gold Coast because the country was rich in gold. Ghana still has some of the best quality gold in the world.

Even as late as the 1970s and 1980s when I was growing up there, I often heard reports of people finding gold on the ground after heavy rains had fallen and caused erosion in certain parts of the country. So it is fair to say that when the British were the sole administrators of the country in those colonial days, they removed much gold. This gold could now be languishing in their treasuries and making the British richer while Ghanaians remain very poor and unable to visit Britain without following strict immigration rules. The same situation might also have happened elsewhere in Africa.

However, unlike the British, who at least gave their former colonies some type of full political and economic independence, the French not only maintained a stranglehold on their so-called former colonies, they cynically and irresponsibly propped up and kept in power some of the most brutal dictators the continent have ever known.

In my own homeland of Togo, the French unequivocally and unconditionally supported the brutal reign of the Black African, Eyadema, for almost 40 years until his death in February 2005. Every attempt the Togolese people made, politically and militarily, to depose this brutal dictator was thwarted by the French.

On numerous occasions, the French sent in their troops to support this useless dictator when it was obvious he had his back against the wall. They also sabotaged all international efforts to rid Togo of this man by persistently recognizing fraudulent elections he held in the face of international condemnations.

One wonders what the French think. But as I continue to argue, these are some examples of racial superiority on the part of the French, which transferred as black racism against blacks because of some of the blacks' collusion with the French. Eyadema was definitely their guy because like many thousands of Africans, he fought for the French in some of their wars to dominate the world – in this case the Algerian War.

When Eyadema returned home and became destitute, instead of venting his frustration on the French who had forced him and others to fight for them, Eyadema and his followers staged sub-Saharan Africa's first military coup. This overthrow opened the door for subsequent military coups in Africa south of the Sahara. That was the only way to appease Eyadema, but it was at the expense of the innocent Togolese people. After this military coup, the Togolese were forced to endure almost four decades of military rule, humiliation, degradation, extreme poverty, unsolved murders and extra judicial killings.

The examples in Togo merely tip the iceberg of the French behaviour in Africa. As I said, the French propped up some of the world's most well-known brutal black dictators, and in all cases the dictators left office or died leaving catastrophic and devastating legacies. In the former Zaire, now the democratic Republic of Congo, the French kept Mobuto Seseseko in power. Although the French knew about Seseseko's excesses and brutal reign, they helped him loot the country's money.

At one point, according to bank statements from his Swiss and European accounts, Seseseko was said to be worth more than his own country. Today, the Democratic Republic of Congo is a devastated country. There is no indication of any economic help from the French or the Belgians (the actual colonizers of the country) for the poor people of the Congo, who are suffering because of the failed French policies.

Their meddling in Rwanda led to what became one of Africa's worst human catastrophes in modern history, following the brutal genocide there in 1993. Another instance was the Ivory Coast, where the French kept another of their black cronies in power. Unfortunately, this crony meddled in the affairs of the neighbouring states. Once again, the consequences of interference resulted in devastating wars, this time in neighbouring Liberia and Sierra Leone.

Unfortunately, the French, who still believe they have the birthright to control the destiny of Black Africans, have not learned their lessons. They continue to meddle and back unpopular and undemocratic regimes on the continent. These regimes are headed by black despots such as Omar Bongo of Gabon, who after the death of Eyadema in Togo took the mantle as Africa's longest ruler.

It is obvious that under no circumstances would the French allow themselves to be ruled by an unelected dictator. So why then do they support leaders who not only oppressed their people, but engaged in abuses of human rights and an iron rule for so many years? For years, the French used stability as their rational of supporting those governments.

But again, events in the Congo, Ivory Coast, Rwanda, Togo, etc., clearly demonstrate that the policy of keeping one man in power for an indefinite period eventually leads to chaos. These people are not infallible and are not going to be in power forever. In effect, the divide and rule tactics they perpetuate to hang on to power becomes a problem after they are gone.

The French also have the habit of trying to preach to Africans to avoid the English language and want Africans to protect the French language and French culture, as if Africans don't have their own languages and culture to protect. Almost every French leader in the past forty years has made these calls to Africans at every Francophone summit.

It is not only my observation that has been critical of these organizations, especially the Francophone.

Here is what Amnesty International had to say in its criticism of the Francophone countries during the latter's 1999 summit in Moncton, New Brunswick, Canada. The human rights group charged that 32 of the 52 member states of the Francophone were guilty of serious human right abuses. It also pointed out that some of the leaders attending the summit would have been barred from entering Canada as ordinary citizens. It asked why a country like Canada, which was spearheading calls for international war criminals tribunal to bring justice to abuses of human rights, can cast a blind eye to abuses committed by some of these countries. It reserved its condemnation especially to countries such as Burkina Faso, Rwanda and Cambodia.[12]

In a rather disappointing reply to the criticism, the secretary general of Francophone, Boutros Boutros-Ghali, responded that human rights discussion would be limited at the summit. He flatly made nonsense of any human rights concerns that were raised. He further pointed out that many of the countries attending the summit were under-developed, and economic development needed to be a priority over human rights. What a pathetic and unfortunate statement from a man who once was secretary general of the United Nations. How dare this man put economic interest above human life and human dignity? Who will be the beneficiary of those economic developments if these leaders continue their genocidal rule unchecked?

It's also ironic to note that the summit, which is billed as a summit to unite the French-speaking world, had many members who have no relationship with the French language. Zimbabwe is a typical example. There is no single history of its nationals speaking French.

Not only are the Francophone and the British Commonwealth, under their current format, unwarranted, from an African perspective, they are also irrelevant because the original idea of visa-free travel among the member states no longer exists. Citizens of countries from the poorer member states now have strict visa requirements to visit the rich members. Besides, economic assistance, which was used as part of the rational to form the two organizations, is something that cannot be justified. The largest donation to the poorer member states from Africa comes from countries such as the United States, Japan, Canada, China etc., which did not colonize any of these African countries. So, I ask, just what benefit have Africans gained by being in these two organizations for the past forty years?

The two organizations have become a stage where irresponsible African leaders showcase their prowess, but in the eyes of rational human beings, their stupidity. First, they spent millions to bribe their way for the opportunity to host the annual meetings of either the Commonwealth or the Francophone. When the African leaders were awarded the opportunity to host the summits, they spent lavishly with their people's limited resources to impress.

Generally, I would have no problem with these institutions, had they not been linked with colonialism and imperialism. I also don't have difficulty with countries such as Canada, Australia and New Zealand being in the commonwealth or the Francophone, as the majority of these countries' populations trace their ancestry to either the British Empire or the French.

Therefore, the two institutions are good for them. Besides, the term Commonwealth fits these countries because they literally do have common wealth. But that is an absurd terminology for member countries of the developing world, because there is nothing commonwealth about them.

Unfortunately, some of the leaders of the poor member countries are corrupt and irresponsible. They used various methods to prevent their citizens from traveling abroad to seek a better life. They used excuses, such as "brain drain," to convince the developed world to stop their own citizens from migrating even though these same leaders have always sent their own children to these developed countries for their education.

They do this, despite the fact that, each year, immigrants of certain countries remit billions of dollars back to their native countries. This does help the economies of those countries and raises their standard of living. Yet there are corrupt African leaders who are not capable of looking after their own people, but still try to prevent them from traveling abroad to make money and make their dreams come true. They also engage in bogus agreements with governments of the developed world, which often leads to their citizens getting deported at random, most often in an inhuman and degrading way. I believe that these corrupt African leaders do this because they know once their people receive a good education and become enlightened, they will exposed their governments' evils.

These corrupt African leaders want to enrich themselves, build super mansions, drive posh cars, and live lavish lives, while the masses remain in abject poverty. When election time nears, they go to the rural areas with rice and sugar to buy the votes of the unsuspecting poor folks. Unfortunately, these short-sighted, selfish and cruel leaders don't want people who will compete with them. They want subjects, and like the old-style monarchies, people who bow and worship them because of their riches and power.

A case in point is Togo's Eyadema, whom I mentioned earlier in this chapter. Before October 1994, the citizens of that country did not require a visa to enter Germany. This enabled many Togolese people to make it to Germany to seek political asylum and to escape Eyadema's brutal rule.

However, Eyadema knew that the large influx of Togolese into an influential and well-established democracy, such as Germany, exposed his evil regime among the European Union countries and other international organizations. So, Eyadema not only made it difficult for the Togolese people to secure travel documents, he also lobbied the German authorities to imposed visa restrictions on Togolese travelers to Germany. In October 1994, the German authorities did indeed do this, thus killing decades of a privilege that Togolese people had enjoyed. This privilege was also a little concession from the Germans for colonizing Togo.

The sad part of all of this is when these people are in power, they consider themselves invincible and infallible; they don't realize they will die one day no matter how long they remain in power, and that decisions they make have long-lasting consequences. Eyadema is now dead, but the Togolese people now pay the price and have to live with hustling for the rest of their lives to secure a visa to visit Germany. And it is all because of one man's foolishness and selfishness. I wonder if any African leader has considered why Mexico, which is richer than any African country, continues to encourage its citizens to migrate to the United States, at all cost, legally or illegally.

When I was in Saudi Arabia, I could not count how many times the Philippines government officials visited the kingdom to lobby for Filipinos to have employment opportunities in the oil-rich Kingdom. By the time I left the kingdom in 1994, every Saudi company, shop or enterprise employed one or more Filipinos. For example, the pharmaceutical company where I worked from 1992 to 1993 had more than one hundred Filipino contract workers at a particular time. Several other companies I knew had over two hundred Filipinos working at the same time.

There can always be talk about debt relief, reparations, economic aid, etc., but not until factors such as the above are considered, and Africans are given the same opportunity as people of other skin color, Africa will forever remain destitute. If free movement of goods and people are not a good thing, why do the rich countries have visa-waiver programs and free trade zones among themselves?

As mentioned earlier, Africans are the people who most frequently have their visa or refugee applications rejected. This again is against the backdrop of historical fact that Black Africans are not known to have a history of terrorism, hijacking, and high-profile hostage-taking cases.

I have also found it disturbing that many Africans tend to pride themselves on being colonized by the English or the French. That has often led to rivalry between the two groups.

This type of thinking was apparent, especially among my Togolese colleagues at our refugee home in Germany. They were so pro-French that they often claimed that everything French was the best. They even had the ridiculous assumption that the French National soccer team had the best jerseys of any country in the world.

Whenever I tried to explain to them the negative impact of colonialism and the unfortunate policies of the French in Africa, they accused me of pro-English bias and attributed that to receiving my education in English- speaking Ghana.

While it is true that I am mainly pro-English and pro-American and, of course, a big fan of the British Monarchy, that is separate from my views about the negative legacy of colonialism or the French policies in Africa, which for decades have infringed on the sovereignty of African countries. Not even being forced to flee their homeland by the regime propped up by the French, could detract my Togolese colleagues from their love affair with anything French.

There also is the foreign aid and loans which are given, unregulated, to these leaders. Apart from the leaders looting the money, they also spent the bulk of it buying weapons. As demonstrated in several parts of Africa, weapons become self-destructive instruments. Some corrupt leaders have also used their countries' scarce money to buy expensive, but obsolete, military hardware. Then they never use the hardware and eventually dispose of it, thus wasting millions of dollars which could have been used to finance and provide good education, good health care, as well as sustaining other much- needed social development projects for their people.

But unless there is consciousness awakening and strong influential advocacy groups from their brethren who are in privileged positions, Africa will continue to be a suffering continent for many, many years to come. No one can dispute that the reality of black history is very painful.

Unfortunately, Africa's holocaust didn't happen for just ten or twenty years. The continent has experienced centuries of brutalities, which in most part were perpetuated by various European colonizers. And in order to awaken the inadvertent among them, Black America needs to change its selfishness and become proactive in every struggle that involves black people everywhere, not only the problems that affect them at home. As mentioned in Chapter Fourteen, Black America as a whole must simply understand that their cause and that of Black Africans are not separate compartments.

SIXTEEN

Intolerance

Like my great grandfather, I am a Muslim and my religion is Islam. I also come from Africa. So, I get hit with racism and other discrimination from three different dimensions: First, I have to fight discrimination because I am black. Second, I have to combat discrimination from Black Americans because I am Black African. Third, I have to fight discrimination because I am a Muslim.

It is important to note that a Black African, who is a Christian, would normally not face discrimination based on religion. Therefore, I am very disturbed by the increasing level of intolerance, particularly among African Americans.

I have heard many blame the anti-Islamic situation on September 11, but that is not the reason for this world dilemma. Anti-Islamic activities have occurred long before the 9/11 attacks. I had several instances in Germany where Black Americans discriminated against me because I am a Muslim. That was during the late 1990s. I get asked all the stupid questions about why I chose to become a Muslim. My African American brothers have made racist and disparaging remarks against Muslims; I sometimes find this difficult to absorb.

One day in late April 1996, three Jehovah Witnesses came

to my refugee home in Koetz, Germany. I knew the leader of the group, which included a female at the refugee reception centre in Neu Ulm. By law, they were not allowed to visit us at our refugee homes.

However, on numerous occasions they had secretly done so, despite the refugees usually shunning them. This day was no different. When they arrived at our residence, my friends locked their doors and refused to allow them in. I saw they were embarrassed and anxious to talk to somebody. I tried to encourage them to leave honorably. But they took advantage of my kindness to talk to them and asked me if I could give them a moment of my time. I agreed to allow them in my room on condition that we kept our discussion to religious dialogue and not an attempt to convert me because that would never happen.

They accepted my conditions so I let them into my room. After initial introductions, the Black American in the entourage was the first to speak.

"How did you become a Muslim?" he asked. "Did you become one willingly or did your parents force you into it?"

This wasn't my first time at the receiving end of this question from a Christian. I knew where he was headed because for years the world propaganda has believed that Muslims are generally forced to accept the religion.

"Before I answer your questions, might I remind you of our commitment – general religious issues only," I said. "If you are trying to convert me, that won't happen. So, let's stick to our agreement and agree to disagree on each other's religious beliefs."

"Fine," they said. All nodded their assent.

And so in plain language I told them my story. I told them that not only were my great grandfather and every member of my family a Muslim, including distant family members; I was also a devout Muslim. At the tender age of 25, I had made my first pilgrimage to the Holy City of Mecca and by the age of 30 had made four more. Multiple pilgrimages are a clear indication of satisfaction with my religion. I also told them that despite being a devout Muslim, I knew the Bible very well thanks to receiving part of my elementary education at a Roman Catholic school. Then I hit them with some personal percentages. Over 90 percent of my friends and girlfriends were Christians. Some of my friends even took that extra religious step to become priests, catechists and evangelists.

"We have kept our ties because we respect each other's religion," I said.

"But what about the treatment of women in Islam?" the young lady in the group asked?

"Open your Bible and read 2nd. Corinthians 14:35."

She did so, including the part where it states women are not allowed to speak in church. When she finished, she looked up at me with a puzzled look on her face.

"Aren't you violating the Christians teachings by preaching to me, since your holy book forbids you from speaking in a Church let alone preaching to me?" I asked.

Then I had her read related quotations from Timothy, etc., and she became more confused and was not able to answer my intense questions.

Then the group leader stepped in to defend her. He tried to mix me up with muddled Bible interpretations. I had heard them all before from my Christian friends. I turned to the young woman.

"Miss, do you know that three Islamic countries, namely Turkey, Pakistan and Bangladesh, have all elected woman prime ministers before? Bangladesh, in particular – it is one of the world's largest Muslim countries and for more than one decade has been ruled by two women prime ministers.

This is an achievement many so-called women-friendly western democracies have yet to do." I pointed a finger at her. "And did you also know that there has since been a woman president in Indonesia, the world's largest Muslim country? Even Iran, of all countries, has elected a woman vice president. In fact, these countries, along with India, which although not Islamic, have the second largest Muslim population in the world and make up more than three-quarters of the overall Muslim population in the world." I smiled at her.

As I had observed many times throughout my relationships with my Christian friends, it was obvious this lady and her friends were ill-informed about Islam. I don't know if it was propaganda to smear Islam or sheer ignorance on her part. But I've always expected those preaching the word of God and doing His work to be honest, truthful and very God-fearing. After all, their preaching impacts their audience, especially when their mission includes trying to convert them to their beliefs.

As our dialogue continued, the young lady was lost in the equation. She remained silent as I continued to bombard her leader with a series of questions.

"Have any of you ever read the Holy Koran or any other authentic Islamic literature? I asked. "Can you give me evidence that thousands of Muslims in the west who convert to Islam were forced into it? May I remind you that Islam is seen there as the fastest-growing religion."

None of them had read the Koran, not even a single paragraph of any Islamic literature. It was obvious all they knew about Islam was hearsay. So the bottom line is, how could anyone preach to me about something he or she hasn't read, especially, when they claimed that their source had come from my holy book?

Finally they left. The young lady looked like she had been

disgraced by a tarring and feathering. She never returned, but the group leader became a frequent visitor, always coming with a different buddy.

That is not the end of the story. As recently as May 5, 2006, I went to a photo studio to get some passport-sized photographs for the renewal of my Immigration papers. As soon as I entered the shop, the owner, who told me she was a Canadian of Korean extraction, began talking to me about religion.

"What religious group do you belong to?" she asked.

"Islam."

She paused for a bit with her mouth open.

"How can a nice guy like you be a Muslim?"

"Why are you saying that?" I kept my usual patience and tolerance. "Don't you know that you are violating Canada's hate crime laws?"

At that moment she realized I knew my rights and wasn't just another ordinary African who could be pushed around. She then switched the whole exchange into jokes. However, she remained adamant about her negative Islamic views.

After she took the snapshots, she asked me to wait for a couple of minutes for the pictures to be processed. While we waited, she started in about herself and a church she claimed to have founded with a white Canadian.

"Why don't you come to one of our prayer meetings because well, you seem like a nice guy?" (She repeated this "nice guy statement over a dozen times during my visit.)

"Sorry," I said. "I'm a Muslim, very happy with my religion and will remain a Muslim until my dying day."

Then she switched to the Africa issue. She began telling me how she liked Africa and its people, how she had invited some Black Africans into her church and how they had become full-time members. She recounted all the places in Africa she had visited. She added she was so obsessed with her love for Africans that she had adopted a very famous Ghanaian name, Yaa Asantewaah. Yaa Asantewaah was a very famous female warrior of the Ashanti tribe in Ghana who fought bravely and led the Ashantis in some of their many wars with the British during the British rule.

Finally, she realized that her tactics wouldn't change me, so she went in the backroom to get my photographs. But in a very deliberate act, which was obviously meant to delay me, the job that should have taken less than 10 minutes took almost 30 minutes.

And in a rather bizarre twist, she kept some of my photos without my permission. I discovered this, because after she had finished processing the photos, I realized the total pictures, which should have been four as I requested, were six. I thought the extra two were a bonus for the inconveniences she had caused me. She cut them to the appropriate size and put them in an envelope.

However, when I arrived home and opened the envelope, I found only four pictures, which led me to believe she had kept the other two. I had seen studio photos of several black males posted on her walls and I hoped that wasn't what would happen with mine. She needed my permission to do this. There was no other reason for her to keep the two photographs.

Unfortunately, these misnomers, misconceptions and misinformation about Islam and Muslims are not limited to this Jehovah witness group and this particular lady, but, and I hate to say it, they are rooted deep in the African American ranks.

From my experience and interactions with African Americans, not only do half-truths and misunderstandings of Islam exist among many African Americans, there is also large-scale intolerance of Islam in their community. It makes me wonder how on earth they think they can fight racial discrimination. No one can eat their cake and have it, too, as the old adage goes, so Black Americans can never accuse others of discrimination when they cannot first clean up their act.

The Bill Cosby saga is one very high profile example. In a blistering attack aimed at poor African Americans at the National Association for the Advancement of Colored People's (NAACP) gala event in Washington DC, May 17, 2004, not only did he make remarks that offended his own people in America, he also made some obviously racist remarks that affected Arabs and millions of Black Muslims who happen to have the name Mohammed. In trying to be political correct, here is what Cosby, the undisputed king of comedies, has to say about African Americans and his resentment of how some parents name their children.

"What part of Africa did this come from? We are not Africans? Those people are not Africans; they don't know a damned thing about Africa." He went on to lambaste parents who give their children names such as Shaniqua, Shaligua and Mohammed. He referred to that as "crap" and then said, "and all of them are in jail."[13] I don't know what Cosby meant by his later statement. Unfortunately, this statement drew loud applause from the largely middle-class African American audience, which he was clearly trying to please.

However, I do know, as a typical West African, the name Bill Cosby is not African, so perhaps he referred to Africa from another planet.

I wonder where all this rage and hatred came from. Don't get me wrong. I appreciate Mr. Cosby's efforts at attempting to show his true African ancestry and remind his fellow lost African Americans of their history and heritage. However, that rage and hatred is not African. Africa needs much support from its brothers and sisters in the Diaspora, but not this kind of bigotry.

It is regrettable how people can sink that low after a meteoric rise to fame and fortune. For years I have been one of Bill Cosby's biggest fans. Sometimes I was so obsessed with his shows; I skipped some very important appointments just to watch them. But his current state of affairs, which also includes endless accusations of sexual harassment, leaves a bad taste in my mouth. I am saddened that he has become a big disappointment to me; I must confess that without reservation, especially with his outburst at this NAACP gala event.

In Chapters Nine and Ten, I mentioned the kind of racism east and West Indians were perpetuating at a company where I worked for several years. Unfortunately, they weren't the only ones engaged in racial discrimination here. My black friends from the Caribbean region and North America also had their own form of discrimination. Most of these dozen or so guys worked part-time. As a Blackman, who lived and worked in the mist of racist West and East Indians, I had hoped for cooperation and solidarity from my black brothers. Instead I found that not only were my black brethren intolerant of Islam, they frequently used racial slurs against the East Indian and the Chinese fellows in the company.

However, it was their hatred of Muslims that tore at my soul. Initially when they were hired, they tended to be friendly and somewhat sociable. But once they asked about my religion because of my name and I said I was a Muslim, they distanced themselves from me. They ignored my friendly greetings. They also had the habit of insulting Muslims every time they visited the washrooms and found the washrooms messy. I use the word "Muslims" because this company also employed many

Sikhs and my black brothers mistakenly believed the Sikhs were Muslim, which they are not. It is important to remind the readers that I was the only Muslim in the company then.

It is a universal truth that Muslims are required to pray five times a day and they must wash before saying their prayers. Unfortunately, as in many public washrooms I have seen, I found an abundance of water and toilet paper lying on the company's washroom floor. It was so grungy that I posted a note in the washroom urging users to flush the toilets after use, and to refrain from randomly flinging paper and water on the floor.

However, my black brethren blamed Muslims because they believed the mess occurred because Muslims have to wash every time they use the bathroom. Some of my black brothers even made the absurd allegation that water was always on the floor because Muslims didn't use toilet paper after relieving themselves.

I never said prayers at work, so I also never used the washroom as they believed. I have always prayed at home or in a Mosque. The only time I used the washroom was in the afternoon after work and only to wash my hands. Because I knew about the washroom's filthy condition, I normally made sure I relieved myself before heading to work. The situation was the same as many other workplaces. The toilet seats were so dirty that the users just stood on them, which increased the filth.

Sadly, one day as I went in to wash my hands, I caught a Jamaican brother pissing on the floor. He happened to be one of the harshest critics of Muslims and people who mess up the washrooms. Before I could ask him why he had done this, he shamefully told me, the extreme cold weather had shrunk his penis and that he was finding it hard to direct his penis inside the toilet seat.

These are some of the unfortunate scenarios about racism. Whether these people were Muslim or not, the stereotypes and bigotry shouldn't have happened in the first place. The reason for this hostility and intolerance among African Americans and these Caribbean blacks is hard to comprehend because I have never seen any documented fact where Muslims have treated African Americans badly. Muslims didn't enslave African Americans and dehumanize them.

Although attempts have been made to link Muslims with the so-called triangular slave trade, we all know where these slaves ended up and who their masters were for over four hundred years. Muslims didn't segregate Black Americans. Islam doesn't portray the image of Devil and Satan as black and God and Angels as white. Apartheid was not a Muslim thing. Nowhere in the history of humankind is there a record of Black Muslims being refused entry into a Mosque or having the mat they sat on thrown away because of their skin color.

There is absolutely no justification for this. This hatred has nothing to do with 9/11; it was there long before 9/11. Muslim nations, through Non Alignment Movement (countries not aligned with NATO or the Soviet Block), have stood shoulder-to-shoulder with blacks and other progressive people in the international community to fight to end apartheid in South Africa. At the same time, Christian Zionists and the neo-conservative Movements (who are nowadays revered by most Evangelical Christians and connected with some Black American Christian evangelists) opposed any sanctions against the apartheid regime in South Africa.

A typical example is United States Vice President Dick Cheney. As a congressman, Cheney staunchly supported the apartheid regime and opposed sanctions against it. In 1986, he voted against a resolution calling for Nelson Mandela's release. I wonder where these politicians would have landed after their destructive actions if these actions been against some other racial groups.

Every time I watch Black American evangelists scream while lambasting Muslims and other religions, I bow my head in shame and ask myself whether they really know their history. These people behave as if Christianity was created after the abolition of slavery, lynching and segregation in America.

Although Christianity recently celebrated its 2000-year-anniversary, whatever evil people have done in the name of Christianity, and any other religion for that matter, could never be eradicated. No reasonable people ever forget their history no matter what its length, especially a history as painful as black history.

Don't get me wrong. I am not against Black America being Christians – far from that. I am only saying that the Back American community needs to remember its history. They need to refrain from getting carried away by misinformation and misconception about other ethnic groups, because this leads them to behave irrationally themselves.

And when they act this way, they diminish any of their genuine grievances. We can't walk both sides of the fence. We can't hate and discriminate against people who do not share our beliefs or skin color while we criticize and call for the heads of those who discriminate against us. The civilized world cannot accept this double standard under any circumstances.

We must either act collectively and aggressively in our condemnation of all forms of racism, hate and discrimination in the strongest terms possible or maintain the status quo and accept them as part of life.

SEVENTEEN

Final Word

People often asked how and why the holocaust happened in Europe. Most often, the answer is blind ignorance. But it is more than that. What happened occurred because of pure hatred and bigotry. And it happened because the world was timid to condemn and act decisively.

If anything, Islam is the only religion that recognizes Judaism and Christianity as Divine religions. It is also the only religion urging its followers to believe in the teachings of messengers and founders of both religions. That is why Muslims cannot insult or say anything bad about Jesus or Moses. The truth is, a Muslim is not a Muslim if he or she does not accept Jesus and Moses as prophets of God, Period. And insulting Jesus or Moses means one is not a Muslim at all.

That is in sharp contrast to insults by some Christian Fundamentalists who shamelessly insult the Prophet of Islam with impunity. Speaking of tolerance, Muslims attend Christian schools, but the reverse has never happened to my knowledge. I am a good example of millions of Muslims across the world who have attended Christian-controlled schools. For over sixty years, Muslims, who make up about a quarter of the world's population, have tolerated the lack of any permanent representation on the United Nations Security Council. This situation means that their interest has not been served. However, despite their tolerance here, Muslims are often accused of being intolerant.

Then there is the Prophet Mohammed, whom many have shamelessly made the subject of their vitriol. Prophet Mohammed is one of the few religious founders who took a firm stand against racial discrimination. That occurred 1,400 years ago during his last pilgrimage to Mecca. He stood on top of Mount Arafat and declared in his last sermon:

"No Arab has superiority over any non-Arab, and no non-Arab has any superiority over an Arab; no dark person has any superiority over a white person and no white person has any superiority over a dark person. The criterion of honor in the sight of God is righteousness and honest living."[14]

The Prophet Mohammed also put these powerful observations into practice during his life and mission. He appointed Bilal, a black man from Africa, as one of his lieutenants and made him the sole caller of the prayer, *"Azhan."* Some supremacists among his influential *Quarish* tribe considered this move a slap in the face. That was 1,400 years ago. Long before the United States was created. Long before slavery was abolished. Long before blacks in America were given their rights.

Isn't it ironic that all these years after Prophet Mohammed made a black man one of his deputies, the Bush administration, and America for that matter, takes pride for installing the first black secretary of state in the country's history?

Generally, whenever I compare the menace of racism to terrorism, people say, "How dare you equate terrorism with racism?" But I say, "Hey, what is the big deal?" Yes, terrorism is a dangerous phenomenon, but by God, so is racism. As dangerous as terrorism may be, historically, its impact on the suffering of mankind is just a fraction of what racism has done to mankind.

Racism is responsible for the slavery of black people. Racism is the only reason for the mob lynching of black people. Racism is responsible for the holocaust, which almost led to the extermination and annihilation of an entire ethnic group. Racism is responsible for the genocide in Sudan and Mauritania.

Millions have perished because of racism, and tens of thousands continue to suffer on a daily basis because of it. The only difference between racism and terrorism is, while racism discriminates, terrorism does not. Hence, the lack of seriousness from politicians to confront racial discrimination with tougher measures the way they confront terrorism.

The bottom line is, until there is the recognition that racism is racism regardless of who perpetuates it, until the philosophy, the doctrine, the teachings, and the ideology that rates one race superior and others inferior is realistically fought, discredited and abandoned, until the color of a person's skin is no more significant than the color of a person's eyes, unless racism is recognized as a menace and battled vigorously the way terrorism is, racial discrimination will forever remain with us.

GLOSSARY OF NON-ENGLISH TERM

Abaaya – Long robe worn by most Muslim women-Arabic.
Addendum- Something added or to be added-Latin.
Akan – Language and people mainly from southern Ghana.
Al-Aqsa – Dome of the Rock-Arabic.
Alagyan – Mini-bus operators in Saudi Arabia.
Arbeitloss – Unemployed-German.
Ashanti – Native people of Ashanti Region of Ghana.
Aswad – Black -Arabic.
Auslander Kriminalitat – Criminal foreigners-German.
Auslander Politik – Politics about foreigners-German.
Auslander Raus – Foreigners get out-German.
Ausweise Bitte – Identification papers, please?
Azhan – A person in charge of calling prayer for Muslim Worshippers-Arabic.
Bayern – Bavaria-German.
Bayern Munchen – Bavarian Soccer Club of Munich.
Bilal – One of the first blacks to embrace Islam.
Brother rrr – This is how many non-English speaking Arabs pronounce "brother."
Bundes Liga – German Soccer League.
Bundesamt – Federal Office -German.
Butagenamo– "Son of a bitch"-Tagalong, Philippines dialect.
Dinka – Native blacks in the southern Sudan.
Donau – River Danube. One of Europe's main rivers-German.
Egal – It doesn't matter-German.
Evangelical Diakonie Werk – Evangelical humanitarian Work-German.
Frau – Lady-German.

Gondo group – Means"fucking group"-India and Pakistani dialects.

Hajj –Pilgrimage. Performed annually by able-bodied Muslims all over the world by visiting Mecca.

Haratines–The Arabicized Africans also known as Black Moors.

Haupt Bahnhoff – Main train Station-German.

Hausa – Language and people, living mostly in northern Nigeria, Niger and parts of other West African states.

Janjaweed – Arab militia which has been terrorizing Sudan's black population. Also means a man with a horse and gun.

Jinn – Evil spirit-Arabic.

Jos – One of the states in Nigeria.

Kaufring – One of the biggest department stores in Germany.

Kotokoli – Language and people of the central part of Togo.

Laissez faire- Casual attitude, indifference-French

Landratsamt – Regional office-German.

Landkreise –Administrative District-German.

Maafi – Not available. No one is there -Arabic.

Madrassa – Islamic School-Arabic.

Manshoor – An Arabic name.

Mina – Tent city in the suburb of Mecca. Populated only during the Hajj Pilgrimage.

Miskin – Poor person-Arabic.

Modus Operandi- A method of operating or functioning-Latin.

MRI – Magnetic Resonance Imaging.

Mummu-Uncivilized or Illiterate person-Southern Nigeria Slur.

Mutawahs- Morals Police-Arabic

Offensichlich Unbegrunted–Manifestly Unfounded-German.
Quarish – Prophet Mohammed's tribe in Mecca.
Ramadan – The ninth month in the Islamic calendar.
Rastafarians – A religion practiced by a large number of people from Jamaica.
Rizeigat – Nomadic people inhabiting part of Darfur.
Samara – Slur used to refer to black people. Used mainly by Egyptians.
Schwarzenegger – Black Nigger-German.
Shara – Arabic for street.
Sheitan – Arabic for Satan.
Sheteen – Arabic for 60.
Social Arbeit – Social work-German.
Staccato- Detached or to cut short crisply-Italian
Tokoroni – Refers to people of black race. Term used mainly in the Gulf Arab states.
Umra – Lesser Pilgrimage to Mecca. Undertaken more than once a year.
Unbegrunted – Unfounded.
Was machts du in Deutschland? – What are you doing in Germany?-German.
Yaa Asantewaah – Famous female warrior who helped Ashantis fight the British.
Yah! Tokoroni; ta al hina! – Hey! Blackman; come here!
Zongos – Areas in cities and towns in West Africa populated by non-native residents, mostly Muslim.

Endnotes and References

Chapter Ten

[1] Fulghum, Robert. All I Need to Know I learned in Kindergarten. New York: Villard Books, 1989.

Chapter Eleven

[2] Charette Janice. "Letter to Editor of Vancouver Province from the Deputy Minister. "Vancouver Province, May 27, 2005.

[3] Class of Immigration by Top Ten Source Countries, 2004. For more information go to.
http://www.cic.gc.ca/english/monitor/issue09/05-overview.html

Chapter Thirteen

[4] Mohammed Isa al Qadeeri. Al-Wattan, Kuwait: April 29, 1989, p 14.

[5] Mercer, John. Slavery in Mauritania Today, London: Anti Slavery Society,1981

[6] Mauritania: Ten Years After the Last Abolition of Slavery, London; Africa Watch, July 1990.

[7] Mahmoud, Ushari Ahmad, PhD, and Suleyman Ali B. Baldo. "Al Daien Massacre- Slavery in Sudan, Khartoum: 1987.

[8] African Charter, Article 2.For charter excerpts see
http://www1umn.edu/humanrts/instree//z1afchar.htm
[accessed Dec. 19 2006]

[9] Soudan Francois, "Maaouiya Ould Taya: "Le Sénégal nous veut du mal,' "Jeune Afrique, January 1, 1990. No. 1513"

Chapter Fourteen

[10] "Football: Johansson apology in race row." London: The Independent, November 16, 1996. See also. South Africans Plan to Protest Over Racist Remarks:-
http://www.anc.org.za/anc/newsbrief/1996/news1118
[accessed May 3, 2005]

Chapter Fifteen

[11] "Arrival of Europeans. "Country Studies. http://www.country-studies.com/ghana/arrival-of-the europeans.html [accessed December 20, 2006]. See also The Asante Wars. http://www.blackhistorypages.net/pages/asantewa.php [accessed December 20, 2006.

[12] For further information on this 1999 summit, see the Amnesty International Library online. http://web.amnesty.org/library/Index/ENGARF570341999?open&of=ENG-TGO [accessed December, 20 2006]

For more information on Francophone, from Canadian perspective, see " La Francophonie: a Community Build on sharing and Dialogue. Canada World view. Issue 5, Fall 1999. http://www.dfait-maeci.gc.ca/canada-magazine/issue05/5t7-en.asp [accessed December 20, 2006].

Chapter Sixteen

[13] Cosby, Bill, Pound Cake Speech. Address at the NAACP's Gala to Commemorate the 50th. Anniversary of Brown v. Board of Education. Washington D.C, May 17, 2004. To read the complete speech, go to http://www.americanrhetoric.com/speeches/billcosbypoundcakespeech.html[accessed September 21, 2006]

To Learn more about African American bigotry, visit: http://www.militantislammonitor.org/article/id/2122 [accessed January 6, 2007]

Chapter Seventeen

[14] Mrs. Ulfat Aziz- Us- Samad. "Islam and Christianity." Presidency of Islamic Research IFTA and Propagation. Riyadh, Saudi Arabia, 1984 p. 89

www.ingramcontent.com/pod-product-compliance
Ingram Content Group UK Ltd.
Pitfield, Milton Keynes, MK11 3LW, UK
UKHW041848190726
13854UKWH00002B/771

9 781412 091053